What Readers Are Saying

"Wow, what a story! An incredible journey from hell to heaven in healing, set in motion by a gift of grace from God. This story can help anyone who struggles with questions about their own faith in God."
- Entrada Publishing

"An amazing story! A journey too difficult to write about or speak out loud! Tracey is changing lives, freeing spirits, lifting hearts. Whatever your dark secrets or hindering obstacles might be, after you encounter Tracey, you will feel whole. Tracey is a gifted storyteller, driven to follow her deepest purpose - letting go of fear so others might let go of theirs. She IS Grace!!"
- Jan Fox, 4x Emmy winner

"Tracey's story is one of hope and healing through circumstances that many would find unimaginable. She is courageous in sharing the details of her life and the work that she has allowed God to do in her heart. Tracey's voice is a much needed one in the church today as many women suffer in silence, believing they are the only ones who have experienced the pain of abuse. For anyone who has walked a similar path, or loves someone who has, this book is a must read."
-Kim Feld, Discipleship Director, New Hope Church

"Out Of The Darkroom, Into The Light is a heart wrenching and incredible true story of how healing can begin through one's faith and trust in God. Tracey Casciano pours out her heart and personal journey in a way that will give others hope, healing, and freedom from abuse. Copies of this book belong on the shelves of every Christian and secular bookstore in the world! Thank you Tracey for your courageous and obedient spirit."
- Nancy M. Davis, Worship Leader

"A special kind of courage is needed to speak honestly about sexual abuse and trauma. Tracey possesses this courage and allows us to step inside her memories, walk alongside her through traumatic experience and the struggle to find healing after it. Her story is entirely her own and also that of countless other victims, men and women who can be empowered by her boldness and encouraged by her story of hope."

-Tori Lane Kovarik poet, artist, and educator; author of <u>Falling Season</u> and <u>The Beautiful Ruins</u>

OUT OF THE DARKROOM, INTO THE *Light*

A STORY OF FAITH AND FORGIVENESS
AFTER CHILD ABUSE

TRACEY CASCIANO

WESTBOW
PRESS®
A DIVISION OF THOMAS NELSON
& ZONDERVAN

Larissa,
Thank you for
your friendship
and support
I am blessed
to have you in
my life!
Tracey

WestBow Press books may be ordered through booksellers or by contacting:

WestBow Press
A Division of Thomas Nelson & Zondervan
1663 Liberty Drive
Bloomington, IN 47403
www.westbowpress.com
1 (866) 928-1240

ISBN: 978-1-5127-1469-2 (sc)
ISBN: 978-1-5127-1470-8 (hc)
ISBN: 978-1-5127-1468-5 (e)

Library of Congress Control Number: 2015916272

Print information available on the last page.

WestBow Press rev. date: 10/21/2015

CONTENTS

ACKNOWLEDGEMENTS

This book started after a lot of praying. Fear and doubt almost got the best of me, but when I realized that I could help others with my story, I knew I had to share it. So many people have guided and encouraged me along the way and I thank God for blessing me with them.

John....I love you and the life we have created together. Thank you for always being there for me.

Bennett, Charlie, Will, and Jack....you make me so proud and I love you more than you will ever know.

Pat and John....your love and support has been a very big blessing to our family.

Heidi....the miles that separate us physically will never matter. You are my soul sister.

Julie, Helen, Nancy, Kim F., and Missy....thank you for being my cheerleaders and encouraging me to follow my heart!

Pastor Rusty and New Hope Church....you helped me find what I was searching for.

My sisters in Christ....thank you for all your prayers and words of wisdom.

Andrea A....without you, this book might not have happened!

Jeanette W....thank you for pouring over my words and helping me create a meaningful manuscript.

Facebook and blogging friends....thank you for all your kind words.

INTRODUCTION

I always thought I would write a book. But I assumed it would be a book about the adventures of raising my four sons. I kept chapter titles in my head and thought of all the anecdotes I would write about. The time #2 son knocked over the condom display. When #1 son, who was potty training, picked up the full potty and brought it to me, emptying its contents all over the floor. Of course I'd have to devote an entire chapter to the time we left two kids at the car dealership.

Oh, the joys of parenting! Raising four children is physically and emotionally challenging, and there have been days when I've wondered how I was going to make it to the end of the week or month or year. During those challenging years, I often felt alone since my husband was busy developing his career and I had no one else to reach out to as a stay-at-home mom with no family nearby. Now that all my boys are older, I have been able to focus more on myself and the future. I often feel a little sad as I reflect on how quickly those little boy years have gone by, but I also welcome what God has planned for me.

So, why this book? After all, it would have been much more fun to write about toddler poop and sleepless nights! Instead, the story I am sharing here is one of a painful past and a difficult journey as I've struggled to figure out who I was and where I was headed. And yet as I reflect on that journey, I have come to realize that my struggles in the past may help others. As I began to write this book, I questioned once again why God had allowed my parents to treat me as they did. I started thinking about all the *what if's* that could have happened along my life, and I am thankful for the path into which God has led me. I believe that He offers compassion in the midst of unjust situations and uses everyone and everything to display His wisdom. I hope I can do the same through this book, because I know it was God who gave me the courage to get to where I am today, and I am glad I took the risk to trust Him.

My journey to where I am today would shock many of my friends. For a long time I had been able to push away memories of being verbally and sexually abused by my parents. But when I was 42 years old, those memories surfaced despite my efforts as I began to struggle with the idea of forgiving my parents. When my father died just six months later, the images and memories from my past that I had repressed (but not forgotten!) emerged, and I was no longer able to shake them off. I felt the memories and emotions boiling up inside of me and had no idea how I was going to handle all of it alone.

From the outside, my life looked perfectly normal, and the last thing I wanted was to allow anyone to know what I'd been hiding my whole life. I was fortunate enough to have a few close friends who loved me and helped me through the process of forgiving my parents and healing. I found myself looking to my Bible for truth and wisdom, and I came to believe more than ever that God has a purpose and a path for everyone, including myself.

I was able to step back and realize that I have persevered despite the physical and emotional pain I have experienced. The fact that I have turned out to be a well-educated, happily married mother of four amazing sons is proof that God had a purpose and a plan for my life. I can see now that I am an example of God's grace, and I feel called to share my story so that others who are struggling with hurt, forgiveness, anger, self-doubt or their current life path will find the hope that I have encountered.

We all have to start somewhere, and the good news is that we don't need anything but our heavenly Father and His Word at work in our lives. The combination of God's Word and our own experiences becomes our personal testimony to the rest of the world. I hope and pray that my story will demonstrate that we cannot be defeated by suffering if we depend on Christ.

"For I know the plans I have for you," declares the Lord, "plans to prosper you and not to harm you, plans to give you hope and a future." Jeremiah 29:10-12 (NIV)

CHAPTER ONE

One Sunday morning in the spring of 2013, I sat in church listening to a friend lead the band in worship. So while I am far from a good singer, I did my best to join in. Next to me, my husband sat smiling and singing, and as I scanned the auditorium, I recognized many faces. I felt welcomed and happy to be there as part of this congregation that had become my church family.

When the worship music ended, I sat down and looked at the program laid out for this morning's service. Before the pastor's message even started, I'd taken note of the title and could feel my heartbeat quicken. *FORGIVENESS* it read in large capital letters.

As the pastor began speaking, I felt as though a spotlight was on me. Nothing else was in focus. The pastor was talking directly to me. He read out a Scripture passage: "If you forgive those who sin against you, your heavenly Father will forgive you." (Matthew 6:14 NLT)

I started sweating and felt as though I couldn't breathe. I broke away my gaze from the pastor and looked around to see if anyone was looking at me. Giving my husband a weak smile, I thought to myself: *How could I possibly forgive my parents for all the pain they caused me as a young girl? They don't deserve it.*

As the pastor's message continued, I began to fidget and move around in my seat. After years of carrying my burden and hurt from a life with an alcoholic mother and abusive father, I didn't want to forgive them. I felt that would be letting them off too easily. By the time the service ended, my stomach was in knots. As my husband and I left the church with our four sons and walked to our car, my husband noticed my silence.

"Are you okay?" he asked me quietly.

I waited until we had arrived back home and had some privacy before I told him, "I think the pastor was speaking directly to me. I am supposed to forgive my parents. But how? Why?"

My husband could see that I was struggling and suggested I go speak to the pastor. My gut reaction was no. I responded, "But then I'd have to tell him everything!"

Though I was panic stricken, I knew I had to ask the pastor how I was supposed to forgive two people who had caused me so much pain. How would I even begin the process after being estranged from my parents for almost sixteen years? So the next day I made an appointment with the pastor. Sitting in his office, I told him about my complicated relationship with my parents. He was easy to talk to, and I shared the physical and emotional pain that my parents had inflicted on me. I told him about the sexual abuse from my father. The years of living with an alcoholic mother. I asked him the questions that had been burning in me for years. "How do I forgive my parents? Do I have to go see them? After all these years how am I going to even start this conversation?"

My pastor was very sympathetic and told me something that immediately made me feel better. He said, "You're not alone."

He then explained that if I forgave my parents, that didn't mean they'd be getting off the hook for their actions. But it would allow me to release my pain and turn it over to God. My pastor suggested I speak with a woman in his office who had a similar past. Telling my story again wasn't easy, but it was refreshing to talk to someone who had faced similar trauma. So after all the years of keeping everything bottled up, I told my story twice in one day.

After I came up for air, the woman gave me a hug and thanked me for sharing. While I wiped my tears, she told me about her own parents. Though our stories are not exactly the same, we had both ended up being hurt by the people who were supposed to love us the most. I asked her what I should do. We both agreed that going to see my parents was not a good idea. I wasn't comfortable talking with them over the phone, so I decided to write my dad a letter.

I felt better as I left my familiar church on that sunny day with a plan to finally forgive my parents. Even though it sounded easy enough, I must have started, stopped, and reworded my letter thirty times. In the letter, I explained that my dad and my mom didn't deserve my forgiveness, but that I was tired of suffering from their actions. I emphasized that I didn't expect anything to change between us. I referenced the Bible and made it clear that the real reason I was choosing to forgive them was because I needed to put my past behind me.

I put the letter in the mailbox and didn't sleep for two days. My mind raced. *Did I put a stamp on it? What if it gets lost in the mail and my dad never gets it? Will he call me? Are we finally going to talk about everything?*

Once I recognized it was not up to me, but up to my dad to respond, a sense of peace hit me. The woman who had encouraged me to write the letter called to see how I was doing.

"I am free," I responded.

I felt that the burden of my past was finally released. As days and weeks passed by, I never received a response from my letter to my dad. I am amazed by God's knowledge that I needed to surrender to the message of forgiveness at that time, as just six months later my father died. I am humbled by my own obedience and am confident to this day that I made the right choice by sending the letter. I can't imagine the potential result that I could've experienced from carrying unforgiveness any longer.

There is a story in the Bible that is a perfect example of this. In Matthew 9:35, we find a woman who took a risk to receive healing from an "issue" of her own. The woman had a physical issue and lived as an outcast. She heard reports of how Jesus went from town to town healing people, and she went to see him. She stood among the crowd and told Jesus her problem. And on that day she heard the words that freed her: "Daughter... Go in peace and be freed from your suffering." (Mark 5:34b)

As I shared this part of my story with a close friend, she noted that our pastor had spoken about forgiveness several other times. So what was different about that Sunday? Although I had heard the message before, I wasn't ready to accept it until that day. I believe that my faith up to that point had led me to a place of trust and desire to be more like Jesus. Our hearts must be open to receive the Word of God, and once we allow it to guide us, our purpose becomes clear. As I reflect on my life, I can see that despite the pain and trauma of my past, God was watching over me from a young age.

CHAPTER TWO

I was born on October 6, 1971, to my parents, Robert and Marian. I was their first and only child, and since I have no brothers or sisters, my parents, grandparents, and friends have had the biggest influence on my life. My father was born during the Great Depression. Since his own father was in the U.S. Air Force, he traveled a lot as a child with his parents and a brother. As a young man, my father was exposed to many cultural events and developed an appreciation for the finer things in life. He attended a prestigious college where he excelled in the areas of science and math. This led him to become a computer engineer.

My parents' relationship was unique as the two of them were very different in many ways. My mother was an only child raised in Illinois at the end of the Great Depression. Her parents didn't have a lot of money, and they did not travel. My mom graduated from high school and moved to Alabama with some of her friends. My parents' story began when they met in a bank where my mom worked as a teller. My dad became a frequent customer of the bank. Eventually he asked my mom on a date.

At this time my dad was working as a computer engineer at IBM. After a short period of dating my mom, he found out that he was to be transferred to an office in Germany. My dad didn't want to leave without my mom, so he proposed. After a short engagement, my parents were married on October 12, 1969, in a civil ceremony with just two of their friends and my mom's parents in attendance. They moved to Germany shortly thereafter, where they lived in a small apartment and had the opportunity to travel around Europe.

Pictures in old photo albums show my father's large stature and dark hair contrasted with my petite, blonde mother. They look happy and young in front of the Eiffel Tower and dining in Paris. After a year in Europe, my parents returned to the United States and lived in New Jersey, where my father worked for a division of IBM. Three years after they were married, while residing in New Jersey, my mom became pregnant with me.

My mom didn't know she was pregnant until four months into her pregnancy. In fact, she had been taking diet pills because she thought she was getting fat. When she finally went to the doctor and found out she was indeed pregnant, her astonishment was enough of a shock that she accidentally drove the car through the garage door when she returned home. I've often wondered just how she felt that day. Was she happy to discover she was pregnant with me, or disappointed?

The two happy people in the honeymoon photos contrast greatly with the man and woman who raised me. My earliest memories take place in the townhouse we moved to in Maryland when I was two years old. For the next seven years, I had a corner bedroom on the second floor with yellow wallpaper on it. Our first Christmas in this house, Santa brought me a "big girl bed". This was placed in the front hallway where I saw it first as I ran to see what was under the Christmas tree. It was on this bed that I collected stuffed animals and wished for a real pet of my own. I was never allowed one, and I was told that the reason was because my mother had allergies.

My parents weren't happy when, at the age of five, I used thumbtacks to put up pictures of kittens over the head of that bed. I remember looking at all the cute kitty faces on the wall and playing a game where I could only pick one. Each time I would

6

narrow my choice down to a particular frisky-looking yellow kitten that I named Daisy.

Next to my room was another bedroom, which my parents set up as a playroom. It was in this room that I played with imaginary friends, because I didn't have many friends come to our house. When I was six, my dad got me a model train set and built a huge platform table for it in the playroom. It was far too delicate for my undeveloped motor skills, and I had no interest in it. Wanting to show it off, my dad would invite the older boys from the neighborhood to come over and play with it. I would get really angry that my dad was playing with them, and my dad would say things to make me feel like a baby, such as, "Tracey can't really appreciate all the time I spent setting this up for her."

I sat under the table and listened while the older boys commented on how nice the train set was. I didn't like being ignored and felt like smashing all the trains they were playing with. I wanted my dad to play with the things that I liked, which I had gathered around me on the floor under the huge train table. I didn't like being an only child. I can remember asking my father when I was about eight years old why my parents didn't have another baby. He told me that my mom had never really wanted to have children and that I was a surprise.

I asked him what my name would've been if I had been a boy. After telling me it would have been his own middle name, Reade, my father added, "To be honest, I really wanted a son."

These two bits of information—that my mother never really wanted children and that my father preferred a son—really impacted me and made me feel sad and lonely. Reflecting on this now that I am a mother, I don't know how anyone could tell their own child something that would make them feel so unwanted.

During those years, I often came home from school to find my mom asleep on the couch with a bottle of some alcoholic beverage on the table next to her. I did not know she was an alcoholic, but I did know deep down that this wasn't "normal". My parents often argued about my mom's drinking. When they did, I would run up to my room and hide under the covers to try to block out their voices.

Still, I can remember fun nights at our house. These were often with Neil Diamond, Kenny Rogers, and Willie Nelson on the record player and the smell of cigarette smoke and stale wine in the air. My mom and I would dance, and sometimes she would fall. I would laugh because she was laughing. My father preferred classical music, but joined in once in a while.

When I was in second grade, I made a friend named Katie. I loved spending the night at her house. Her mom was very nice and gave me hugs and tucked us in at night. Occasionally she asked me questions about my mom and how often she drank. I felt uncomfortable and tried to avoid her questions.

Then one day while I was at home with my parents, some men in suits came to our house. My mom was yelling and upset, and my dad seemed worried. I was told to go to my room. Though I went obediently to the top of the stairs, I tried to hear to what was going on downstairs. I heard some more yelling. My mom was demanding to know who sent the men to our house.

When the men left, I heard my mom ask my dad, "Who sent them here? They can't take her, can they?"

I later asked my dad who they were. He told me not to worry about anything. But the next time Katie asked me to come over, my mom refused to let me go. This all made me feel sad and guilty that I had done something wrong. Now that I look back on this as an adult, I realize the men must have been from Child Protective Services. This is one of the many pieces of the puzzle that made up my young life.

As a young girl, I wasn't very confident. My wardrobe consisted mostly of brown, and my mousy brown hair was cut so short that I was frequently mistaken for a little boy. This broke my little girl heart. I begged to get my ears pierced so that people would know I was not a boy.

"No, that's something gypsies do," my mom responded.

A photograph from a Halloween party in an old photo album says it all. There I am, dressed as a mummy, staring longingly at my best friend, the beautiful ballerina. I remember asking for two things every Christmas: a pink canopy bed and a little brother or sister. I never got either. My mom said canopy beds just collected dust. And why in the world would I want a pink one?

As an only child, I became independent at an early age. I walked to elementary school alone or with a group of kids. I would walk to swim team at our neighborhood pool. I have memories of walking with a friend all the way to a local Seven-Eleven to buy gum and candy to take with us to the pool. I'm sure my mom had no idea we'd gone that far.

My mom stayed up late at night drinking and would often be asleep until the late morning hours, so I was usually on my own for breakfast before school. One fun activity in elementary school was having sleepovers with other girls. My mom discouraged me from inviting friends over, perhaps so her drinking wouldn't be discovered. But I was always excited to go to someone else's house. How amazed I was that other moms made fresh pancakes in the morning!

Sometimes after a sleepover, I would get to stay on and go to church with my friends. To me this was a big treat. I liked the smell of churches and the pretty stained-glass windows and enjoyed getting dressed up for the event. I thought churches were magical, and since I had no idea how to pray, I would just close my eyes tightly and clasp my hands together during prayers, hoping that no one would notice my ignorance. When I came home on Sunday from one such sleepover/church adventure, my parents were in the kitchen.

"Why don't we go to church?" I asked them.

They responded, "We don't need it."

I didn't know what that meant, so I continued, "But I like it! It's beautiful. Did you go to church when you were a kid?"

My dad answered, "Yes, going to church was important to my parents. But not to your mom and I."

I learned later in my life that both my parents had indeed attended church in their growing-up years. My dad had been raised in the Episcopalian denomination and my mom in a Baptist church. My dad had even been an altar boy and had received a lot of religious education. I can't help but wonder if my life would've been filled with more happiness if we had gone to church.

Reflecting now on these early years of my life is like watching a movie. I find myself disbelieving that it was really me, although I know it was. As I look at my youngest son, I wonder what his memories will hold. Unlike me, he is a confident, happy kid who knows he is loved by his family and God. I hope that he will remember the good times and try to create lasting family memories.

My parents' choice to not introduce religion into my life impacted the choices I made as I got older. As I look back now, I am confident that God was watching me from a young age and had His hand on me, guiding me towards Him. He knew my heart was where it needed to be, and He never gave up on me. I believe that God will wait for us to come to Him, and when we do, He embraces us no matter how long it has been. He doesn't mind if we've messed up in the past. All He wants is our heart and a relationship with us. We can see proof of this in the Bible, specifically in Psalm 34:18: "The LORD is close to the brokenhearted and saves those who are crushed in spirit." (NIV)

CHAPTER THREE

During the years we lived in Maryland, I enjoyed spending time with my grandparents. My paternal grandparents, Mimi and Fred, lived in California my entire life, so I didn't see them very often. Mimi wasn't my grandmother's actual name, but when I was young, I couldn't pronounce her real name, so she became Mimi, and Fred was Fred.

We flew from Maryland to visit Mimi and Fred in California when I was about seven years old. Someone who had grown up with my dad was getting married, and my parents and I were invited to attend the wedding. Traveling on an airplane was very exciting. I sat next to the window and tried to focus on the clouds as I heard my parents begin to bicker. I didn't know why my dad was asking my mom if she was going to be able to walk off the plane. He motioned towards the small bottles that were on her tray, and she told him to shut up. Of course I know now the bottles contained liquor or wine and am thankful that it was my father who drove us to my grandparent's house.

I hadn't been to Mimi and Fred's house since I was a baby, which I didn't remember, so I had fun exploring. Mimi gave me a tour of their hallway wall, which was covered with photographs from floor to ceiling, and told me who all the people were. I learned stories about my great grandparents and great aunt, and I enjoyed seeing my dad and uncle as babies. One particular picture stood out to me—a black and white photo that hung at my eye level. In the photo, a young man in overalls stood with his arm around a beautiful woman. The couple in the picture were looking at each other and laughing. They seemed happy and in love.

"Who are they?" I asked my grandmother.

She smiled. "That's me and your grandfather when we were dating." Then she bent over and whispered in my ear, "He was pretty handsome back then, wasn't he?"

Several times during our stay in California, my dad mentioned that my mom wasn't feeling well. He didn't seem overly concerned, but on the morning of the wedding, everyone was busy getting ready when we suddenly heard a loud noise from the living room. My dad and grandparents hurried in to see what the sound was. As I came down the hall, I saw my mom lying on her back in the living room, her body shaking and foam coming out of her mouth.

I had no idea what was happening, but was very scared. As the ambulance pulled up outside, I ran back into the guest bedroom where we were staying. I never did get to go to the wedding. The rest of our time in California was focused on trips to the hospital and making sure my mom was okay. Though I didn't know it at the time, my mom had suffered a grand mal seizure as a result of alcohol withdrawal. The scene from that morning is still clear in my memory to this day.

My mother's parents, Mac and Louise, lived in Virginia, so we saw them more regularly. I called them by their first names as they didn't like being called Grandma or Grandpa. They came to our house for holidays and birthday celebrations, and I was always excited if they brought a gift, especially if it was in a large box. These large boxes held beautiful dresses with matching purses that Louise would pick out for me. As soon as I pulled the dress from the box, I would run into the bathroom to put it on, then model for everyone. These were very special to me since my mom always dressed me like a tomboy and kept my hair as short as a boy's.

But the only time I wore these nice dresses was with my grandparents. I would spend the night sometimes at their high-rise apartment. Louise always called me her "pretty little lady" and made me feel special. As I soaked in my grandparents' large tub filled with bubbles, I was able to forget about how much my parents fought.

Louise was a beautiful woman who had red painted fingernails, always wore skirts and high heels, and smelled of flowery perfume. When I emerged from the luxurious tub, she would wrap me in a soft robe and invite me to her dressing table. As I sat in front of an illuminated mirror, she would blow dry my hair with a big, round brush. This was all very special for me, and I loved the attention. When I emerged from the bedroom, my grandmother would announce, "Presenting the Princess of the Bathtub!"

My grandfather would then burst into cheers and applause. He was a bit mysterious to me as he was missing part of his index finger. I made up stories in my head as to what had happened to it. I imagined that he'd shut it in the car door. Or had it bit off by a dog. Or was cutting carrots and accidentally chopped it off. I eventually found out that he'd lost it in an accident at work involving a large paper cutter.

But for the most part, my grandfather Mac was a quiet man who would invite me to sit in his lap as he drew beautiful cartoons for me. When it was time for me to leave, he would slip candy in my pockets. This made me giggle as he would whisper, "Don't tell your mother!"

I enjoyed these times with my maternal grandparents. Then one day when I was in the fourth grade, I came home from school to see that my mom had been crying. I was scared when she told me, "Your grandmother Louise had a stroke."

I was only ten years old and didn't know what that meant, but I had a bad feeling. I knew Louise was in the hospital and that I wouldn't be able to see her for a while. I tried to listen and understand my parents' hushed whispers over the next few days, but didn't understand what was happening to my grandmother.

About two weeks later, my parents told me we were going to visit Louise. I let out a shriek of excitement upon hearing the news. By this time, my grandmother had been moved from the hospital to a nursing home. As we drove to the nursing home, my parents prepared me for what I was going to see. "She looks different than when you last saw her... Don't be upset if she doesn't talk to you... She can't walk anymore."

My imagination was spinning as we entered the building. A smell of mashed potatoes and human waste immediately filled my nose as we walked down a long hall. We turned into a room, and I saw my grandfather standing at the end of a bed. I saw that he was crying, and as I looked at my grandmother, I understood why. The woman in the bed only slightly resembled my beautiful grandmother. I was scared and filled with questions. My parents encouraged me to give Louise a hug, and as I did, I noticed that she now smelled like chemicals instead of perfume.

My parents continued visiting my grandmother every weekend. Though I begged them not to make me go, they insisted. My grandmother now looked like a different person. Her blonde hair had turned grey and wasn't styled as I had been used to seeing it. The right side of her body was paralyzed, making the side of her face droop. Each time we returned home from a visit to the nursing home, I pulled out a photograph from the prior Christmas of Louise standing next to me and promised myself that I would remember her as she looked in it.

About a year after her stroke, Louise developed pneumonia and died. My mom bought me a new dress to wear to the memorial service. As I sat in the church in that ugly white dress with brown stripes, I cried, remembering our special times together, and wondered what Louise would say about my ugly dress. Not long after Louise died, my grandfather Mac moved to Florida to live with another woman. My mother was very upset, and I was sad that I would no longer see him.

We didn't see Mimi and Fred often, but when they did come to visit, it was a big deal. I was in third grade when Fred's sister, whom I called Aunt Judy, died. We were still living in the townhouse in Maryland at that time, and she lived in a house in Virginia. My grandparents flew in from California for the funeral. In preparation for their stay at our house, my mom demanded that I clean my room, help polish the silver, and stop biting my nails.

Aunt Judy's husband had died when I was younger, and they'd never had any children, so my grandfather Fred was the executor of her estate. By this time my father had left his job as a computer engineer at IBM and had started working at a computer company in Virginia. After discussing with my grandfather how a move to Virginia would mean a shorter commute to work, my father was able to get a "family discount" for Aunt Judy's house. A few weeks after the funeral, I was told we would be moving from Maryland into Aunt Judy's house. So the summer before I entered fourth grade, we packed everything from our townhouse (except the train set, which was sold at a yard sale), and moved to a suburb of Washington D.C., in northern Virginia.

Two years after we moved to northern Virginia, Mimi and Fred came to spend Christmas with us in what had previously been Aunt Judy's house. While they were visiting, we went to museums and toured Washington D.C. It was during this trip that Mimi introduced me to God. Looking back, I can see my faith as it developed in stages, similar to the life cycle of a butterfly. At this point in my life, my faith was just beginning, or in the egg stage. When it was time for me to go to bed, Mimi would come in my room at night, and we would say a prayer together. I was uncomfortable when I first started talking to God.

"I don't know what to say," I told Mimi.

Mimi encouraged me to talk to God as if He was sitting on the end of my bed. I remember asking her, "How does God hear everyone's prayers?"

"God is like a large umbrella over the entire world," she explained to me. All these many years later, I think of my grandmother and smile on rainy days.

The good news is that God isn't just there on rainy days. He's always with us during sunny or cloudy days. On the sunny days when life is good, we can thank Him for all that He has provided us. On days that are cloudy and raining, we need to remember to go to Him first with our prayer for guidance, direction and understanding. Looking in the Bible, we can see that God never promised us there wouldn't be bad days. But He did promise us that He will never leave us or forsake us. He promised that NOTHING is impossible when we follow Him. He promised that He will work out everything for our good (Romans 8:28). He promised us that His love for us is steadfast and unfailing. All we need is faith!

CHAPTER FOUR

I was excited when we moved to Virginia, thinking this was going to be fun and an adventure. Being still a young girl, the scary part for me was that my grandfather's sister had died in that house. Before we moved in, I noticed a large painting of Aunt Judy hanging in her bedroom, which was now to become my parents' bedroom. In the painting, Aunt Judy was looking straight ahead and smiling. I felt as though she was watching me. But by the time the movers had brought in all our furniture, the painting had disappeared from the bedroom wall.

One afternoon my mom asked me to retrieve something from a closet in the basement. When I opened the door to the basement, I screamed. There was Aunt Judy staring at me and smiling. It was actually the painting, but I was sure the house had ghosts and wouldn't go into the basement alone for several months. Eventually I met a girl who was my age, and we became fast friends. I showed her the painting. When I started fourth grade at the local elementary school, she told our other classmates that there was a ghost in my house. Consequently, I never had a single sleepover at my house.

The weather in northern Virginia can be beautiful, but the summers are hot and humid. My parents fought and argued about the thermostat constantly. My dad would turn on the air conditioning, and then my mom would immediately turn it off, saying, "It's too expensive."

This battle went on all summer long. When my dad was home, my parents were arguing. My mom's drinking was by now an all-day event. I would see her in the kitchen pantry, trying to hide that she was pouring wine in a cup. She hid the cup and alcohol bottles behind food items, but my dad and I knew they were there. My dad would ask me if I knew how much she was drinking each day. I told him that if I came around the corner unannounced and saw her, she would quickly put the cup down and try to hide it. She was often angry for no particular reason, and it seemed like she was always yelling at me. The hot, humid nights were unbearable, and even with a fan I would wake up soaked with sweat.

I wanted to get away from my mom and out of our house, so I spent my summer days at our local pool and became a pretty good competitive swimmer. My mom would drive me to our neighborhood pool and sit in the sun with her friends. One day I asked her for some of the water in the thermos she brought every day.

"No!" my mom told me. When I asked why, she replied, "Go away, and stop bothering me."

Defiantly, I waited until she went to the restroom, then removed the top of the thermos. I immediately smelled the alcohol. I looked around the pool deck and wondered if all the moms brought wine to the pool, but suspected they didn't. After our time at the pool, we would go home, and she would fall asleep. She would wake up in a terrible mood, yelling at me for various things. "Why didn't you water the lawn? How long are you going to let your clothes sit in the washer?"

I had no idea how to make her happy and felt like I was always walking on egg shells. Life at my house in the summer was miserable. We didn't go on many trips or vacations. But there was one special trip that first summer after we moved to Virginia when we went to an amusement park and made plans to spend the night in a hotel. I was thrilled!

At the park I went on rides with my dad, but my mom said she wasn't feeling well. I noticed that her hands were shaking. Five hours after we arrived, we were sitting in the First Aid office because my mom had another seizure from alcohol withdrawal. I was scared and embarrassed. I didn't understand what was happening. After a day at a local hospital, we headed home and didn't get to spend the night in the hotel.

My dad was not only a computer engineer, but also a part-time photographer. We had a darkroom in our basement where he developed and printed his own film. In order to maintain the chemicals and photographic paper, it was necessary to keep them cool. So the darkroom had a small air conditioner in the window. My dad was furious that my mom would not let him turn on the air-conditioning. One evening after a yelling match with my mom, he took his pillow and began sleeping on an air mattress in his darkroom.

I have no idea why my dad didn't stand up to my mother. I started complaining that it wasn't fair he got to be in the air conditioning while I had to suffer. After I expressed myself, my dad suggested I bring my own pillow into the air conditioned room with him to sleep. At first it was fun, like camping inside. Then he started touching me. It was in that dark, cramped room that my abuse started.

Trying to remember something you've forced yourself to forget for a long time is physically and emotionally draining. As I've worked through my feelings towards my dad, my emotions rise as I remember being young and adoring him, then change to a sickened disgust as I remember the details of my abuse. I was now eleven years old. Even at that young age, I knew deep down that what we were doing was wrong. If I questioned it to my dad, he just responded, "We both love each other, right? Then no one is getting hurt."

I felt trapped, conflicted, and alone. I was desperate for my father's attention and love. I was scared of what might happen if someone found out. Therefore, I didn't tell anyone.

During tough times in our life we often ask, *Where is God?* Where was He when that little girl in the darkroom needed Him? We can turn to the Bible to help answer questions like this. In hard times when you cannot see God's hand, you must trust His heart and know for certain that He has not forsaken you. When you seem to have no strength of your own, that is when you can most fully rest in His presence and know that His strength is made perfect in your weakness. As the Scripture says, "My grace is all you need. My power works best in weakness." (2 Corinthians 12:9 NLT)

CHAPTER FIVE

As part of my dad's photography business, he took photographs of homes for realtors to use in their advertisements. Every weekend we filled the car with his equipment and headed out. I would be the navigator with a big atlas in my lap. I enjoyed this time with my dad, and we developed a strong relationship as we talked during our drives. The houses we went to were very large, and I remember feeling excited as we drove up to each of them. While my dad set up his equipment, I would explore the grounds.

I loved going into the back and finding a large pool. I'd imagine myself swimming and relaxing if we lived there. We had access to the insides, and I would run from room to room, picking which would be mine. For a few short hours, I was able to enter a fantasy world where I lived in a big, beautiful house with no drinking or fighting.

During these trips, I'd also talk to my dad about my mom's drinking. I asked, "Why doesn't she want us to use the air conditioning or the heat?"

He'd just shrug his shoulders and sigh. Then he would look at me and try to make me feel better by saying, "I'm so lucky to have you. I'd have gone crazy a long time ago if it weren't for you."

I loved this attention, and it made me feel loved. Even all these years later, my heart races as I reflect on this. My dad was just as desperate for love and attention as I was. Unfortunately, he got it from me, his daughter, in inappropriate ways. When I was in the 6th grade, I started wearing a bra. I was mortified that people would know and begged my mom not to tell my dad. That first evening that I had it on, he came up behind me and snapped the back of the bra. Ashamed and embarrassed, I ran into my room crying.

Later he apologized, "You are turning into a beautiful young woman."

Of course I instantly forgave him. As the weather turned cooler, the nights in the basement turned into nights in my parents' bedroom. My mom would usually pass out on the couch after too many drinks. A few times she would wake up and begin banging on the door, which my father would always lock.

"I know what you're doing in there!" she would yell at us. "I'm calling the police!"

My dad would reassure me that my mom wasn't going to call the police, but I was scared. If my dad got in trouble and left, what would I do? The next day we would all act as though nothing had happened. My mom never talked to me about it, and it became a dark secret.

Our days went on as if nothing was abnormal until one evening when my mom was driving me home from a school event. When I got into the car, I could see she had been drinking. I felt helpless as we approached a stoplight and slammed into the car in front of us. I flew forward, my head hitting the windshield. When I noticed the large crack in the windshield, I instinctively felt my forehead for blood.

As the driver from the other car approached our car, my mom glared at me and said, "Don't say a word!"

I wanted to tell the other driver that my mom was drunk, but knew that I couldn't. Later that evening I told my dad what had happened. He was furious. Shortly after that incident, my mom went to a rehab clinic. It was during the time of my mom's absence that I realized my life was not normal. I was paralyzed by my fears. What if my mom died and I was left with just my dad? What if something happened to my dad and I was left with my mom?

As I reflect on this time in my life, I have many mixed emotions. I feel sad for my young self and angry that I didn't know God yet. During those years I felt so often alone and afraid. I know now that fear is part of human nature. We have a fear of rejection, fear of missing out, fear of being different. We can look for examples in the Bible of overcoming fear with our faith and belief in God. In 1 Samuel 17:8-11, David's fear holds him back as the Israelites try to go against Goliath. Later we see that David was held back by those around him (1 Samuel 17:26-29) who didn't think he was strong enough to take on Goliath. David was also held back by his lack of preparation (1Samuel 17:39).

But David was able to conquer these fears and defeat Goliath. So why do we let fear control what we do or don't do? Our faith is like a shield in battle, made of impenetrable material. When we have our faith as our shield, God will protect us from our fears. I would learn this many years later.

CHAPTER SIX

My mom's stay in the rehab clinic didn't prevent her from a relapse. During my middle school years (7th-8th grade), my mom's drinking became worse. My dad and I began measuring the levels on the hidden bottles to try to figure out how much she was drinking each day. She lost her temper quickly with me and became more physically violent, even starting to hit me.

One night at dinner I said, "Mom, I can hear your jaw click when you chew."

She became furious. Picking up a crystal dish full of sour cream, she slammed it onto my head. I was surprised, and aside from the pain of the cut crystal digging into the top of my head, I was embarrassed. Of course, as a typical adolescent girl, I also worried about my hair. My mom and I both stormed out of the dining room, leaving my dad to sit at the table alone.

My mom and I began arguing and fighting often. She would go into fits of rage for no apparent reason. One argument we had over and over again was about the temperature of our house. In the winter she would not allow the thermostat to go above 68 degrees. She and my father would argue over the cost of the heat. My father would eventually give up and either go to work or walk into his home office, turn on a space heater, and shut the door. I was always cold and begged her to allow it to go to 70. I would sneak down the hall to turn up the thermostat. If I got caught, she would slap me across the face.

One day I was in my room with the door locked. When my mom demanded that I let her in, I retorted, "No!"

My mom then pounded on my locked bedroom door with a hammer. Not only did this leave a large hole in the door, but the mirror on the inside of the door shattered. When my dad came home from work, he was angry at the destruction she had caused. She often slapped me across the face, and at times I would beg my dad to divorce her.

She continued hitting me, and one day when I was fourteen, I hit back. She was stunned and began to cry. I felt terrible and ran away to a friend's house. I begged my friend's mom not to tell where I was. But of course she did.

Later that evening my dad came to pick me up. I don't remember the conversation we had in the car or what happened with my mom when I returned home. But I remember having a feeling of being trapped. I felt like I had two lives—the life outside of my house and the life inside it. At school I was seen as a good student and had many friends. I got good grades and made people laugh during the school day. But when I went home, I was measuring alcohol levels in bottles in our kitchen pantry while being abused by my mother and sleeping with my father at night.

Thinking back to this time still makes me feel so angry. I remember the helpless feeling. I wanted to get out of my situation, but I was trapped. If I told someone, I didn't know what the repercussions would be. I was scared, so I used what little knowledge I had from my visits to churches with my friends and from what Mimi had taught me and started praying for help, asking God to protect me. At the time I didn't really know if it would work, but figured I had nothing to lose.

There are times in our lives when we can feel helpless and afraid of our current situation. As followers of Jesus Christ, we can look for help in the Bible. In the book of Job, chapter 5, Job is desperate and needs protection. He has lost all his wealth, his home, and his ten children. He is sick with a horrible disease. He even wishes he could die.

His friend Eliphaz responds to Job's wishes to die. Eliphaz encourages him to go to God, rather than relying on fate. "If I were you, I would go to God and present my case to Him. He does great things too marvelous to understand." (Job 5:8-9 NLT)

The book of Job goes on to describe Job's arguments and reasons for doubting that God is going to protect him. God replies to Job and challenges his wavering faith. In the end, Job acknowledges his own ignorance, and God blesses him in the second half of his life with twice as much as he had lost (Job 42:12-17).

Though I didn't know it at the time, but I too was like a Job. I had no one else to turn to. At least that is what I believed.

Chapter Seven

I don't know exactly how or why the abuse from my father stopped. As I think back to that time, I can't recall a specific event or conversation with him about it. But by the time I entered high school, he was no longer approaching me at night. I, in turn, did my best to put my memories of those nights with my father behind me. I began socializing more with boys and felt more confident once I no longer had to worry about my father's abuse. My relationship with my father became instead one of denial and avoidance.

I continued this relationship with my father, so that our relationship looked "normal" on the outside. I made the freshman cheerleading squad and had a new group of friends who didn't know me from elementary or middle school. I felt confident I could survive four more years at my house with my parents. My dad spent a lot of time at the office, and I became busy with school activities, so I didn't see him much. My mother was still drinking, and we argued and fought a lot. I had a few older friends who could drive, and I avoided being at home with my parents as much as possible. Life was getting a little bit better.

One spring night that freshman year as I went to bed, I was frustrated to hear my parents arguing again. Pulling the covers over my head, I went to sleep. I was awakened suddenly in the middle of the night by a very loud noise and screaming. I lay in my bed with my heart pounding as I heard my dad moaning, "Oh no! Oh, no!"

Running to the hallway, I saw my mom in a heap at the bottom of the stairs.

My dad was assessing her condition and asking her questions. "What did you take? How many?"

I stood stunned as I listened to my dad call the 911 operator. "My wife has overdosed on sleeping pills and alcohol and has fallen down the stairs."

I heard my mom slurring the words, "I want to die! I want to die!"

I don't think I moved until I heard the sirens. Realizing the neighbors would hear the noise, I panicked. As the responders loaded my mom onto a stretcher and into the ambulance, I began making up stories in my head to tell my friends. Then it hit me. My mom had just tried to kill herself! I was scared, mad, and ashamed as I realized that she wanted to leave me.

Once the ambulance left, my dad called my best friend's mom, then drove me to their house before heading to the hospital. I couldn't go back to sleep. Despite an offer to stay at my friend's house, I was adamant that I was fine to go to school the next day.

So I went to school and acted as though nothing had happened. I decided that if anyone asked, I would say that my mom had tripped and fallen down the stairs. Not a big deal. I was in history class when I was notified that I'd been given a pass to go see my counselor.

"I've spoken to your dad," the counselor told me. "I know what happened last night."

I was so confused and upset that I started crying—not because of what had happened, but because I didn't want my counselor to think badly of me. I begged him not to tell anyone. He recommended family counseling for me and my dad, but we never went. My mom stayed in a rehab facility for a couple weeks. I was hopeful that this time it would work, but it didn't.

My sophomore year was easier in some ways. To fit in I needed certain clothes and a certain look, so I babysat and saved my money. I bought designer jeans, got my ears pierced, grew my hair long and dyed it blonde. I was a class officer and involved in many clubs. I wanted to be part of the in crowd, so I went to parties, drank beer, and began dating boys. I did it all and eventually became part of the popular crowd.

During my junior year of high school, I was once again a cheerleader. I never felt more proud than the day I wore my cheerleading uniform as I went to get my driver's license on my sixteenth birthday. During the winter I was on the swim team and developed a serious relationship with a boy. He was on the dive team, and we had practices together.

I had an average-sized body, but was not as slim as some of my teammates. My dad made a comment about some of my female teammates. Then he patted me on the stomach and said, "It looks like you have more to worry about than just the competition in the water."

I was furious and felt ashamed of my body. Shortly thereafter, I began waking up before school every day and doing aerobics. I would eat an apple and two rice cakes for lunch, then go to swim practice for two hours. I was so exhausted after practice that I would go home and get in bed without eating dinner. I began lying about what I had eaten during the day and making excuses for why I wasn't hungry. I weighed myself every day and would stare in the mirror at my imperfect body.

My exercise and eating (or lack of eating) habits continued into the spring. That summer I was a lifeguard at the pool I had gone to since fourth grade. The first day the pool opened, several parents of my friends came up to me. In concerned tones, they asked me, "What happened? Are you okay?"

At first I had no idea what they were talking about. Then I heard one man say, "She's so skinny!"

His comment didn't bother me; on the contrary, I was about to enter my last year in high school, and I felt great. I was finally in control of something in my life. My eating disorder continued for the next year. At 5'4" tall, I had lost twenty pounds and when I left for college, I weighed only 98 pounds.

My story is just one example of how our insecurities can prevent us from being happy. Insecurities can come from the trials we are put through as well as our physical appearance. Our clothes, hairstyles, and concern with image can consume us and keep us from experiencing the life that we are meant to have. In the New Testament, the apostle Peter addresses this very subject in his first epistle. In 1 Peter, chapter one, he gives advice for those who are "God's chosen people." (1Peter 1:1, NLT) He advises us to be truly glad with what we have and to "remember that the heavenly Father to whom you pray has no favorites." (1:17)

As for our insecurities with appearance, the apostle Peter reminds us to focus on beauty that comes from within rather than being concerned with outward appearances: "Don't be concerned about the outward beauty of fancy hairstyles, expensive jewelry, or beautiful clothes. You should clothe yourselves instead with the beauty that comes from within, the unfading beauty of a gentle and quiet spirit, which is so precious to God." (1 Peter 3:3-4)

CHAPTER EIGHT

While my classmates cried at our high school graduation, I felt joy that I had survived life with my physically and, most recently, emotionally abusive parents. My mom often insulted me and made me feel inadequate. I found that after the physical abuse stopped, my father was never easy to please. As acceptance letters to colleges arrived, he was quick to say that another school was better.

The summer after I graduated from high school, I counted down the days until I was able to leave my past. I accepted an offer to attend Virginia Tech, a large university with a rural campus in southwest Virginia, where I would be almost a five hour car ride from home. I was invited to attend an orientation weekend for incoming freshman from high schools in northern Virginia who would be attending Virginia Tech in the fall. We learned the school cheers, talked about what to expect, and I got to meet some other students, including a good-looking young man named John Casciano.

When move-in day finally came, my parents and I drove the 4 1/2 hours from our house to the campus. I couldn't stop smiling. As my parents helped me unpack and get my dorm room set up, I was anxious for them to leave. When we hugged goodbye, I felt a wave of relief. I was finally on my own in a new place and could put my past behind me. I did my best to have a normal relationship with my parents, including weekly phone calls, and we all acted as if nothing had ever happened that was out of the ordinary. This false relationship continued for many more years.

I explored the large campus and was happy to see some familiar faces from the orientation. One of the faces I recognized was John Casciano. We began meeting each other after classes and in the dining hall. We got along great and had some things in common. Although John was a "military brat" (his father was in the U.S. Air Force) and had lived all over the world, we had both graduated from high schools in northern Virginia, were both only children, and had similar interests.

One day John invited me to go out for pizza with a group of other people. Since I was still battling with my eating disorder, I panicked at the thought of eating with John and his friends. Fearing the calories a pizza would have, I told John, "Um, I'm allergic to tomatoes."

Returning alone to my dorm room, I was furious with myself. Fortunately, John called me again. For our first official date, we went dancing. We soon became inseparable, studying together and going to parties together. John also helped me get past my issues with food. He made me feel special and appreciated me. By the time our first fall break came, I was crazy about him.

We had told our parents about each other, and since we both lived in the northern Virginia area, we thought it would be fun to go out to dinner with our parents while we were home for the fall break. My issues with food were much better, although I was still exercising a lot. But as my parents and I drove to the restaurant, I began to panic.

What were you thinking? I said to myself. *My parents are not normal.*

My mom was nervous too. To calm herself, she drank too much alcohol during our restaurant meal. She began slurring her words and needed my dad's assistance to walk to our car. I was embarrassed, ashamed, and angry as we left the restaurant. But to my relief, when I talked to John the next day, he didn't say anything about it.

Returning to campus, John and I finished out our first semester and had a wonderful time together. During our first Christmas break, John and I spent a lot of time together. After a few more meals with my parents, he soon realized that my mom had a problem with alcohol. He never asked me any questions or made me feel uncomfortable, and for that I loved him even more. As we spent more time together, I learned that he was raised as a Catholic but that his family didn't attend church regularly. By the time we finished our freshman year, we were totally in love with each other.

When we each headed back to our own homes for the summer, we were separated by a thirty minute drive. John and I made a plan to see each other as much as possible. We both had summer jobs, so we spent weekends and holidays together. At the end of the summer, we both returned to Virginia Tech. We had requested to live in the same (co-ed by floor) dorm building, and to our delight, John and his roommate were assigned the room directly above me and my roommate. The four of us had a great year together. I enjoyed my classes and started thinking about a future career in advertising.

When I returned home at the end of my second year, I was able to get a summer internship at a local advertising agency. The job wasn't quite as glamorous as I had hoped, but I learned a lot about the business, and it kept me away from my mother during the day. I had suppressed my memories with my father and was able to have a superficial relationship with him at this time.

John and I saw each other often during the summer, and I got along very well with his parents. They invited me to go to the beach with them at the end of the summer, and I was ecstatic. My parents and I had never rented a house on the beach, so this was a new experience for me. I enjoyed being with John and his parents very much. The four of us had a great time on the beach during the day and visiting sights and restaurants in the evenings.

At the start of my junior year in college, I moved off campus and into a townhouse with two other girls who were good friends of mine. John and his roommate rented an apartment just down the street from us, and we continued spending a lot of time together. I was happy to have my own bedroom and finally got my yellow kitten named Daisy. She climbed the curtains, ate my roommate's goldfish, and hid jewelry in the couch. But I loved her, and she made me feel that I'd finally gotten something I had wanted so badly from my past.

My two roommates and I got along very well and had fun going to parties and activities together. But unlike me, my roommates would get up and go to church on Sunday mornings. This bothered me and made me feel inadequate. I was angry at my parents for not teaching me about religion and felt ignorant. I wanted to ask my roommates questions, but didn't know what to say or how they'd react. I knew that John was raised Catholic, as his Italian parents had been, and I was embarrassed that I knew nothing about God or the Bible.

"Why don't you go to church on Sundays?" I asked John one day.

He seemed surprised and responded, "I attended as a child to prepare for my First Communion ceremony and confirmation into the Catholic Church. But beyond that, our family really only goes to church on holidays."

After I explained how I felt, John suggested we go to church together. I was nervous and scared he would think I was dumb, but trusted him enough to go with him. We began going to a Catholic church, and John showed me stories in the Bible. It was exciting for me like a new course in school with a very cute professor. Thinking about my earlier analogy of the butterfly, I consider this to be the larva, or caterpillar, stage of my journey to a relationship with Jesus.

One day during this time, my dad called me. He said, "Guess what? I got a new job, and your mom and I are moving to Massachusetts."

At first I didn't know what to think. I'd never been to Massachusetts before, and now instead of being four and a half hours from home, I would be a plane ride away. Once it sunk in, I was thrilled that I would never have to go back to the house in Virginia again. I told myself that the past was over and done. I'd closed and locked the door to that part of my brain which held so many awful memories. Now I could live a normal life, or at least pretend to do so.

At Virginia Tech, the usual practice when classes ended for a semester or the holidays was for the majority of students, including all my own friends, to leave campus and return home. Since my parents were paying for my tuition, I felt obligated to visit them when I had the opportunity. So that year for our holiday break, I reluctantly flew from Virginia Tech to Massachusetts to be with my parents in their new home in a suburb of Boston.

My parents met me at the airport, and we drove to a nice neighborhood of large colonial style houses. Their new house was larger and much nicer than our house in Virginia had been. When I first went inside, I was surprised to see that my parents had a large black cat living with them.

"I thought mom was allergic to cats!" I commented.

"The cat's been around the house every day since we moved in, and we were worried it was lost," my dad explained, "He stayed on our front porch, so we decided to feed it. Then it got cold, and we were worried he'd freeze, so we let him in."

I felt angry and hurt to discover my mom wasn't really allergic to cats. She just hadn't wanted me to have one. Here I was twenty years old, and I was jealous of a cat who had won my parents love and attention!

Being in a new place, I had nothing to distract myself with when my mom once again started drinking too much. As I lay on my bed in the unfamiliar house, I realized something and sat up with a jolt. The heat was on, and I wasn't uncomfortable as I had been during our winters in Virginia. How was it that so much had changed? I felt myself becoming bitter towards my parents as I remembered the deprivation of my younger days in our house in Virginia.

Of course, I was thrilled when John came to visit me in Massachusetts for the first time. He arrived after Christmas, and the two of us went into Boston and enjoyed exploring the historical city together for a few days before he returned to Virginia. Once the holiday break was over, I packed my suitcase and was excited to return to school. I was carrying my bags down the few steps from the house into the garage when my parents' new cat ran between my legs and made me trip. I fell, badly twisting my ankle. As I cried out in pain, my dad came over to me and helped me get up.

"We really need to go," he said, "or you will miss your flight."

I wasn't sure I could walk, but I gingerly placed weight on my injured foot and hobbled to the car. I somehow managed to get through airport security and to my boarding gate, feeling relieved to be away from my parents again. As I settled into my plane seat, I tried to ignore the throbbing pain in my foot. The flight from Boston to the small airport outside of Virginia Tech is about 3 ½ hours. By the time we landed, my foot/ankle was very swollen. I tried to stand up, but I was absolutely not going to be able to walk.

I explained what had happened to a flight attendant. He arranged for someone to carry me off the plane, then settle me into a wheelchair. John was going to pick me up at the airport, and we'd made plans to meet at the baggage carousel. Once I'd been brought down to the baggage area in my wheelchair, I looked around for John. By then my foot was hurting badly, and I started to cry. When John saw me in a wheelchair and crying, he was very concerned. Once I'd told him what had happened, he responded disbelievingly, "Your parents put you on an airplane knowing that you were hurt?"

John drove me to the local hospital. An x-ray confirmed I had broken a bone in my foot. Using a pay phone at the hospital, John called my parents to inform them of the situation. When he returned to me, I was getting a cast put on my leg. I could tell he was annoyed by his conversation with my parents. During the next few months I spent on crutches, John was very kind and helpful. Though I had a difficult time navigating the large campus, I was able to continue attending all my classes.

For the rest of that school year, John and I were together as much as possible. When we weren't studying, we had fun going to concerts, restaurants and parties around campus. That next summer, I did not want to return to my parent's house in Massachusetts, so I stayed in Virginia and continued to live in the townhouse I shared with my roommates. I took some summer classes on campus and worked at a frozen yogurt store to have some extra money. I was happy that I didn't have to go back to Massachusetts, and by the end of the summer I could make a perfect waffle cone!

John went back to his own parents' house in northern Virginia to work for the summer, but we were able to talk on the phone several times a day. Even though I missed him, I enjoyed a nice summer on my own. Continuing our relationship of denial and avoidance, I spoke to my parents every Sunday. These conversations were usually directed by my father who talked about himself, his new job, and how he was feeling.

After three years of hard work, our senior year of college came at last. As much fun as it was, recognizing that this was our last year brought the reality of the future into clear focus. John wanted to go to law school, and we knew we wanted to be together, so we started talking about where he should apply.

This was an unsettling time, but since John and I had been attending church together, I prayed and relied on God to keep us safe and lead us in the right direction. I would express my nervousness to John. He would always smile and respond with confidence, "Everything will work out."

At this time, John's father was in the U.S. Air Force, so we weren't sure where his parents would end up living. Sitting on John's bed, which was covered with brochures from different law schools, John and I discussed the options.

"How about Atlanta?" I suggested.

John replied, "If we're going to go to a totally new place, wouldn't it be good to know at least one person?"

Then he added, "How about a law school in Boston? At least then we would be by your parents."

I cringed inside, but didn't know what to say. As far as he knew, I had a pretty good relationship with my parents. John and I had dated each other for all four years of college, but I had never told him about any of my "stuff". So John applied to law schools in Boston and was accepted to New England School of Law in the heart of downtown Boston.

CHAPTER NINE

On a sunny day in May, the class of 1993 was rewarded with degrees from the various colleges that make up Virginia Tech. I received a Bachelor of Arts, and John received a Bachelor of Science. Mimi and Fred flew from California for the event, and John and I celebrated with them, our parents and friends.

Mimi surprised me with a beautifully wrapped large gift. I opened it to find a scrapbook filled with letters I had sent to her and Fred from a very young age. It was fun to read some from when I was a young girl, and I was touched that she had kept them.

My parents had driven their car from Massachusetts, and John and I were to follow them back. As I packed my belongings from the townhouse I'd live in for the last two years, I was suddenly very emotional and filled with doubt about my choice to go with John. I didn't have a job and would be living with my parents until I could find one. The plan was that I would work and save some money to get an apartment in the city to be close to John.

The next morning, I wept as I said goodbye to my roommates. John and I loaded all our belongings and my yellow cat Daisy into a rented truck, then followed my parents' car the long distance to Massachusetts. John stored the items he would need for law school in my parents' garage and helped me get settled into my new room in their home. We had one weekend together in Massachusetts before he flew back to Virginia, where he would live with his parents and work for the rest of the summer until law school started.

I cried when John left and wished the summer to pass quickly. I felt alone in a new place with no friends or job and was miserable to be living with my parents again. The next three months were truly awful. Having been away at school, I was used to having freedom to do what I wanted. Now suddenly everything I did was under a microscope. My mom drove me crazy, and I found myself getting very angry. If I left my bedroom to go downstairs for a drink of water, she would pop into my bedroom and turn off my light, as though to see what I was doing.

Every day I scoured the newspaper, made phone calls and applied to advertising firms in the area, desperate for a job opportunity that would allow me to leave the house. My mom was still drinking as well, and this led to more fighting between my mom and dad in the evenings. Meanwhile I was also trying to avoid my dad's awkward hugs. My only relief was to stay as busy as possible and out of their presence.

Feeling desperate, I finally took a job that I didn't like and started to save some money, focusing on my goal of being on my own again. When John came back to Boston in August, he immediately had a roommate, law school friends, and an apartment. I was a little resentful and once again felt trapped. I was desperate and knew that I had to get out of my parents' house quickly.

John and I tried to see each other as much as possible, but were separated by a forty minute train ride from my parents' house in the suburbs to his law school campus in the middle of Boston. After three months of working, I had saved some money and was ready to move out. John and I met with a realtor and looked at apartments that were close to his own apartment. Living in the city is not inexpensive, and when I returned to my parents' house to tell them I'd found an apartment, they expressed anger that I was simply wasting my money. My mom made hateful comments about John while my dad seemed hesitant to co-sign the lease for me.

I in turn was very confused. With all that had happened and their negative attitudes towards me, why would they want me to stay with them? I panicked as I realized that I needed them to agree or I'd be trapped with them once again.

I was relieved when my dad finally did sign the lease, albeit reluctantly. On a hot, humid day, I moved into my tiny studio apartment in a beautiful, historic neighborhood of Boston called Beacon Hill. My parents, John, and I sweated through our clothing as we carried my belongings and furniture up three flights of stairs. I refused to let my mother's complaints or my father's criticism of the old building burst my bubble of happiness.

I loved my tiny studio apartment. I decorated it all in pink with flowers everywhere. For the first time in my life, I lived alone (except for my cat Daisy) and felt great. I got a new job that I enjoyed much more than the last. This necessitated me taking the train each morning into the financial district of Boston. During the week, John went to classes at New England School of Law while I was at work, but we would see other in the evenings. Our apartments were just a few streets apart, which made it easy for us to meet often.

My job didn't pay very well, and I figured out quickly that if I was to pay my rent and other bills and still having some spending money left over, I needed to get a second part-time job. So three nights a week I was a hostess at a local Italian restaurant. Even though this made for some long days, I really liked it. John and I made some great friends and loved living in the city.

During our first winter in Boston, there was record snowfall. We watched the snow pile up along the city streets and were amazed that it didn't melt until April. Without cars to worry about or driveways to shovel, we didn't care. We put on our boots, coats, and hats and lived life to the fullest. John would meet me at the end of my shift at the restaurant, and I would emerge into the cold with a bag of fresh, hot rolls. We would walk hand in hand in the silent snow enjoying the buttery warmth of the fresh bread. I kept my distance from my parents, and my life was really good. Once again, I thought my ugly past was behind me and felt proud of myself.

During John's second year of law school in Boston, we started attending a Catholic church at the bottom of the hill in the neighborhood where we both lived. We also started to talk about a future together. While we were attending the church, I was very much still a novice believer, focused more on memorizing the required prayers than actually trying to understand what they meant. I started daydreaming about a wedding and imagined myself floating on a cloud of white silk as John and I danced together as Mr. and Mrs. Casciano.

That fall, the alumni association from Virginia Tech sent invitations to a formal New Year's Eve party at a hotel in northern Virginia. John and I coordinated with mutual friends to meet us there. On the morning of New Year's Eve, we flew from Boston to Virginia, where we were happily reunited with our college friends.

At the party, I arranged for our group of friends to meet at midnight under the balloon drop that would signify the arrival of the next year. John and I had a tradition of telling each other our resolutions during the countdown to New Years. There we all were dressed in tuxedos and sparkly gowns, awaiting the start of a new year. As the countdown began, the crowd was so boisterous that John had to shout over the noise, "What is your resolution?"

I announced loudly in his ear, "I resolve to balance my checkbook this year."

John laughed and suddenly bent down. Annoyed that he'd picked that time to tie his shoe, I shouted, "Get up, it's almost midnight! What is your resolution?"

John looked up at me with a smile and said, "Mine's a little better than yours."

Pulling a ring box out of his pocket, he went on, "I resolve to marry you."

As the balloons fell around us, our friends cheered. I hugged John and cried. It was an absolutely magical night, and I was filled with joy.

We returned to Boston happy and in love. Once back, we began making plans for our wedding, honeymoon, and future together. I had already begun to dive into bridal magazines and clip out pictures of flowers, dresses, cakes, and veils when John asked me about getting married in a Catholic church. I was confused by his question, since I'd already assumed we would. I hadn't realized I'd need to be baptized and receive Communion in order to be married in a Catholic ceremony, and I was suddenly worried that this was going to delay the process. My perception of faith and what it mean to be a Christian were still very naive at the time, and to be honest, self-serving.

John and I went to see the priest in the church we'd been attending. When we told him our exciting news, he assured me our getting married would not be a problem. I began meeting with him weekly to prepare for being baptized and taking First Communion. Every time I opened the Bible, I became more comfortable with it and more confident. As I read the New Testament, I learned about Jesus and wanted to know more about His story.

On a beautiful Sunday morning that spring, I was baptized and received First Communion with John at my side. As I looked out across the congregation, I was pleased to see that my parents had come and were supporting my decision. I felt wonderful as members of the church came up to me to offer their congratulations and welcome me into their congregation. I finally felt as if I belonged in a church and was truly a child of God.

At this point, I was still learning and developing my relationship with God. But as I looked back at my past life from that day I was baptized, I could clearly see that He had been watching me and waiting for me. For this, I thanked God regularly.

John and I began really sharing our faith as a couple after attending a weekend retreat called Engaged Encounter. At the retreat we read scripture together and talked about God and what our future together would look like. We made a promise to each other that we would continue seeking God for advice and wisdom in our married life and raise our future children with an understanding of His love. I had entered the chrysalis phase of my butterfly metamorphosis!

My memories from these years after college are bittersweet. As I experienced a new phase in my life after graduation, I faced many trials with my parents and wanted so badly to put the past behind me. I found myself questioning my past and how/why it had happened to me. Unable to find answers, I pressed on, hoping that one day I would mature enough in my faith and understanding to make sense of it all. Only because of that faith and determination was I able to focus on my goals, stay patient, and persevere.

The Bible discusses the trials that we may encounter in our lives. Many times we want to ask God to make our pain and difficult circumstances go away. As human beings, our nature is to want instant gratification. We look for a quick fix. Diets to lose weight fast. Plans to make us rich quick. Plastic surgery to erase our age.

But what happens when our plans fail? In the New Testament, the apostle Paul explains how our faith will bring us joy even when we are faced with difficult times. "We can rejoice, too, when we run into problems and trials, for we know that they help us develop endurance." (Romans 5:3, NLT)

CHAPTER TEN

My daydreams, clippings from magazines, and favorite scenes from romantic movies all came together as John and I began to plan our wedding day. We wanted a traditional ceremony with our friends in attendance, so we decided to have the ceremony and reception on the military base in Washington, D.C., where John's parents lived.

John's mom was a big help as I began to realize that planning a long distance wedding was pretty stressful. Picking out a wedding dress was something that I had imagined since I was a young girl. In the movies, the bride-to-be comes out of the dressing room, and her girlfriends all break into cheers and tears at how beautiful she looks. I made an appointment at a bridal shop in Boston and invited a friend and my mom to come. The night before the appointment, my friend called to let me know she had a terrible cold and wouldn't be able to go. My mom called me a few minutes later to tell me it was much too snowy and cold for her to come.

I was disappointed. But the next morning I was still filled with excitement as I walked into the bridal salon. However, as I emerged from the dressing room wearing the dress I had always dreamed of, no one was there to tell me I looked beautiful except the sales woman. I tried not to let this dampen my spirits. Instead, I called my parents that evening to tell them the good news. "It's beautiful! There is lace on the bodice, capped sleeves, and a full tulle skirt with delicate pearls."

My disappointment increased when my mom responded, "Don't get too excited. How much is this marshmallow fluff going to cost us?"

Even though my parents were paying for most of the wedding, I didn't invite them after that to give any input to the other details of our wedding. John and I selected flowers, a cake, and the food with only his mother's help and opinion. Our wedding fun was in full swing with showers and parties at work, and John and I were counting down the days until our big day. Then just two weeks before the wedding, my dad called me one evening. I was stunned when he told me my mom was in the hospital.

"She's had a stroke," my dad explained.

Images of my grandmother flashed in my mind, and I argued, "But she's only forty-nine!"

The truth was that years of cigarette smoking and alcohol abuse had made my mom a perfect candidate for a stroke. I was scared and confused, but I felt much better after John and I prayed together that evening. The next day John called his parents and told them my mom had had a stroke. When they questioned how this could have happened, he explained that she had an issue with alcohol, but I suspect they already knew.

Between working and going to the hospital to visit my mom, I wasn't able to concentrate on the final details leading up to our wedding. My dad and I worried that my mom might not be able to make the trip from Massachusetts to Washington, D.C. Fortunately, my dad talked the doctor into letting her go, and just two weeks after my mom's stroke, John and I were married in a chapel on the military base by a Catholic priest.

August 13, 1994, was a hot, humid, wonderful day. The chapel was decorated in white and pink and smelled like fresh roses. One of John's friends helped my mom to her seat shortly before my dad escorted me down the aisle. As I walked down the aisle, I saw our friends, John's parents, and their friends. I saw my mom in the front row. She had a glazed, far away stare, and I wondered if she would remember the day. Sitting next to her were my grandparents, Mimi and Fred, who had come from California to be a part of our special day.

As I looked ahead down the aisle, there stood John in his gray morning suit next to his father and three of our friends. Fighting back tears, I felt pure joy. Our wedding was a traditional Catholic ceremony. At the end, the priest invited us to kiss, not once, but three times, to represent the Father, Son, and Holy Spirit. Our reception was a blur of congratulations and picture taking.

I was a girl who had dreamed of my wedding day for years. Now with the blink of an eye, the day was over. As we arrived at our hotel room that evening, my face hurt from smiling all day, and I was sad to take off my beautiful gown. Looking at myself later in a mirror, I realized that my dream had come true. I was now excited about my new role as the wife of my best friend. The next morning John and I left on a flight to California, where we boarded a cruise ship and had a wonderful week exploring different destinations.

Once John and I returned from our honeymoon to begin our new life together as husband and wife, we moved to an apartment outside of Boston about thirty minutes from my parents. I felt an obligation to have my parents over for dinner once in a while (and it also gave us an excuse to use all our beautiful wedding gifts). My mom had benefitted from some physical and occupational therapy, but was never the same after her stroke. Her cognitive functioning and vision were impaired, and she was much slower physically. She could no longer drive or cook for herself and relied on my father for many of her needs.

This made me feel even more distant from her. John and my dad had a good relationship, but as we spent more time with my parents, it bothered me that John didn't know who my dad *really* was. He didn't know how much pain I had suffered in the past. But how could I ever tell him? What would he think of me?

Then one evening in our second year of marriage, it happened. My parents were over for dinner, and we were telling jokes. John started to tell one that we had recently heard about a little girl and her dad in the shower. When I shot him a look, he broke off. An awkward silence followed. Then I said, "That's not really appropriate."

Surprised and offended, my dad responded, "Come on, it's not like we're children!"

I quickly changed the subject and the evening went on. Later, John asked me what was going on. I hadn't thought about those days in Virginia for a while, and I'd had enough space from my parents throughout recent years that I'd been able to keep my memories locked up until that point. I panicked and tried to make up some answer, but then I started crying. Really crying.

Putting his hand in mine, John said, "Tracey, what is it?"

I knew that I had to tell him the truth. It was very difficult, and I felt as though I'd been dishonest in not telling him before. I was so scared, but I knew I couldn't go on pretending anymore. I felt the pressure of my secret had reached its boiling point, and something had to give. So that night I told John about my past with my father.

My fear of rejection had led me to a point in my life where I was alone with a secret. I felt guilty because of my past, yet unable to share my pain. At this point, I wasn't mature enough in my faith and relationship with Jesus to know how to ask God for help. I was relying on myself and it wasn't enough.

We know that guilt, shame, and pride are all human feelings. In the Bible we see that God sent Jesus to earth to live life as a human so that He could experience life as we do. Our sin separates us from a life with God. God knew this and sacrificed His only Son so that we would be free of our sin. All God wants us to do is trust that Jesus is the path to remove our sin so that we can be close to God. We must not let our human sin, whether it be a feeling or an action, separate us from God. The Bible gives us this wonderful assurance, "For the wages of sin is death, but the free gift of God is eternal life through Christ Jesus our Lord." (Romans 6:23, NIV)

The night I told John about my past, he held me and we cried together. It was the worst and best night of our two year marriage. I told him that I was tired of pretending my relationship with my parents was normal. After that we avoided my parents' calls and invitations while we tried to sort out what this meant for us and our relationship with my parents.

It was harder than I thought, and when we could avoid them no longer, it was awful. I slipped right back into my fake, happy daughter act, but John couldn't play along. He was angry, and his attitude towards my parents had visibly changed. The next time we were together with my parents, I didn't know what to do when my dad pulled me aside and asked, "Is John mad at me? Did I offend him somehow?"

I certainly couldn't be upset with John, but his behavior was making everything even harder. We tried to keep our distance from my parents and made excuses for not being available to see them. But this created a sense of tension. I wondered to myself, how long would this go on? Maybe I shouldn't have told John.

Not long after that, John and I both felt relieved when my dad called us to announce that he had received a job offer with a large software company and that he and my mom would be moving to Utah in a few months. After they moved, I felt the same false sense of freedom that I'd had in the past when I was in college. However, they continued to call and were not totally gone from my life.

I didn't know what to do. I knew that unless I totally cut them out of my life, this cycle wouldn't end. Being a people-pleaser with a big sense of guilt, I felt that I couldn't just cut them off entirely. I felt like I owed them something because they were my parents and had given me a home, clothes, food, not to mention paying for my education and wedding.

So I sent Christmas and birthday gifts and called my parents on holidays. This cycle of pretending everything was okay, ignoring the past, and continued frustration went on for many more years. I tried to push away my feelings and worry by busying myself with work, projects, and fun with friends, just as I continued to hide behind a mask of happiness. As I realized that the distractions weren't helping, I began praying that God would give me the tools to get past my past and move on.

Looking back, I can see that God was working on me during this time. I was so used to feeling guilt and shame from my past, that I didn't even recognize how it was holding me back. I wanted so badly to let go of my feelings of inadequacy and guilt, but had no idea how to do so. Wrapped up tight in my chrysalis, my understanding of what it meant to be a follower and a child of God was still that of a novice. Now that I attend church regularly, read the Bible, and have shared my story with others, I understand that God was working in me to move me away from this guilt and into His grace. I believe that God placed people and situations in my life to help me do this.

It took me a while to get it, but now I see that it's okay if we can't get over all our struggles at once. God just wants us to remain with Him and to grow in the grace and understanding that He provides (2 Peter 3:18). Once we are able to turn our fears and worries to Him, it becomes easier to get past our guilt, and we are able to live a life full of grace and freedom.

CHAPTER ELEVEN

After countless long nights and lots of studying, John graduated from law school. A few months later, he passed the bar exam. Shortly thereafter, he landed a job at a law firm in Boston. I was very proud of him. We celebrated our third anniversary, and John and I began talking about starting a family.

Just a few months later, John and I discovered to our delight and excitement that I was pregnant. We decided that our growing family needed more space and began looking at houses in the suburbs of Boston. That spring, we purchased a small, Cape Cod-style house and found ourselves happy, first time homeowners.

Just a few months later on May 22, 1997, John and I became parents to our first son, Bennett. It was an amazing experience, and we couldn't have been any more proud as we bonded with our little bundle. John's parents came to visit us shortly after we got home from the hospital, and his mom stayed for a week to help me get my bearings.

Looking back now, we laugh about some of our experiences with Bennett (his first bath) and how nervous we were. I was completely in love with our new baby, and although it was overwhelming at times, I enjoyed my new role as a mother very much. As my maternity leave came to an end, I began to panic. I couldn't imagine leaving our son with someone else for an entire day.

Sitting down together, John and I calculated the cost of daycare and other expenses. Thankfully, we decided it was more economical for me not to return to work. Our world changed as we loved this child with all our heart. I remember how much joy just watching him sleep brought to me.

We had Bennett baptized in the local Catholic church we were attending. I was determined to give him a life full of God such as I had never had. John's parents came to visit us several times during our first year as parents and were just as in love with Bennett as we were. We talked to my own parents about twice a month. My dad started asking when we were going to visit them, insisting it was too hard with my mom's situation for them to travel to see us. In response, I used the excuse that it was too expensive and difficult to travel with a baby. My dad tried to make me feel guilty by reminding me that he and my mom had flown me all the way to California to meet my own grandparents when I was only three months old.

I tried not to let this bother me, but it did. As I developed a group of friends who were also new moms, the topic of grandparents would come up. When I explained that my parents hadn't met our son yet, I received looks of disbelief.

Several months later, my dad called to tell me that he had a business trip in Boston. I panicked when he added, "Since I'm going to be in a weeklong conference, I thought your mom could stay with you guys and just hang out with you and the baby."

I felt trapped, but didn't have the guts to say no. I wondered: *How am I going to manage a baby and my mom?* The days leading up to their arrival were very stressful as I tried to imagine how I would deal with seeing my parents again and having my mom stay at our house.

When my parents arrived, my dad immediately set me on edge by making a disparaging comment about the small size of our new house. The first days with my mom were horrible. Not only did she wet her bed, she also fell down several times, and wanted to hold MY baby! I found a sense of protectiveness towards our son like that of a mother tiger rising up inside me.

One day my mom left her cigarette lighter in her pocket. I thanked God that I discovered it in the washer before it ended up in my gas dryer. I didn't trust my mom to be alone with Bennett for even one minute. By the time John came home each evening, I was an exhausted, emotional wreck. My dad came over only once, claiming he was too tired at the end of a day of conference activities to come for dinner.

Unsettled to see me so upset, John insisted I needed to tell my dad what was happening. So on the fourth day, I called my father on his cell phone and demanded that he come and pick up my mom. I explained that I was not able to take care of both her and a baby. He did so, if reluctantly. But even after they left, I felt very angry with my dad. It was clear to me that instead of having an interest in seeing his grandson, he had simply taken advantage of me so that he could get away from my mom for a few days.

Twenty one months after our first son was born, John and I welcomed our second son, Charlie. I had never felt so happy and blessed. Both John and I loved parenthood. Although we weren't as neurotic or nervous as we were with our first son, our lives revolved around being parents to our two wonderful boys.

When our second son was four months old, we took the boys to visit John's parents in Virginia. We had lots of fun with them, taking the boys to parks, restaurants, and playing together. John's parents began questioning why my parents hadn't visited again and why we didn't go see them.

We made excuses, and I told John's parents that my mom was back to drinking. I'd been left with a very bitter taste in my mouth after my own parents' visit to see us. My dad called me occasionally to tell me my mom had fallen due to too much drinking or to complain about how unhappy he was. Instead of sympathizing, I found myself extremely irritated. I resented that my dad felt a need to burden me with their problems. But instead of letting him know how I felt, I would find myself rationalizing that he didn't have anyone else to tell. *At least my parents lived far away,* I comforted myself.

Sixteen months after Charlie's birth, in July, 2000, John and I had a third son, William (how did that happen?). This was a difficult time since I now had three young children, and Charlie was turning into a very active toddler. Thankfully, I had a great group of friends. One morning as my friends and I were heading with our children to the zoo, I can remember breaking down into tears. I felt totally overwhelmed. I found myself resenting John's job and begged him to come home early every evening. Of course for a young attorney, this wasn't doable, and my pleas began to put a strain on our marriage.

Fourteen months after our third son was born, on September 11, 2001, the terrorist attacks on the United States occurred. This event really scared John and me. His parents were our only real family, and they lived an airplane ride away from us. We now had three young children, and it was clear that I needed help with them while John was establishing his career.

After discussing the situation with John's parents, we took a leap of faith, sold our house, and moved back to Virginia. It was hard to leave our friends, but we felt it was the best thing for our family. We put all our belongings except toys and clothes into storage and moved in with John's parents. Looking back, I can see how difficult it must have been for them to give up their quiet lifestyle and make room for us. I hope that I will be selfless enough to do the same for our boys if asked some day.

John stayed behind in Massachusetts for a few weeks to sell our house and wrap up his work. I navigated a new neighborhood, looked for preschools, and found fun activities to keep my kids busy. Though a difficult time for our family, I know God was watching out for us because John got an amazing job just weeks after moving to Virginia. By then we'd been living for four months with John's parents. As our "holiday season" with them came to an end, I recognized just how lucky we were to have such wonderful grandparents in our sons' lives.

We moved into a house in a great neighborhood just thirty minutes from John's parents and found a nearby Catholic church to attend. Life with three young boys continued to be an exhausting job, and at times I felt like I would go crazy (this time period is the source of those anecdotes for my prior-mentioned original book idea). Our middle son Charlie was almost uncontrollable. Only later would we would learn about ADHD.

Each day Charlie presented me with a new challenge. One simple trip to story time at the library ended up at the emergency room when Charlie tried to run away from me in the parking lot. Trying to restrain him, I pulled him by the arm, but ended up dislocating it at the elbow.

Nor could we go to a park that didn't have a fence around it for fear of Charlie running off. Many times I had to leave Bennett, who was only four years old himself, to watch baby William while I ran off to catch Charlie. By this point I was exhausted and felt helpless.

Finally at a routine doctor's appointment, I broke down into tears. When I explained how my stress was affecting my relationship with my husband, the doctor recommended I see a therapist and get some part-time help at home. I had never been to a therapist before, but knew I needed something to help me feel more in control.

Desperate, but afraid, I went to see the therapist my doctor recommended. Once I'd explained to the therapist how my hyperactive son was going to be the death of me, she began to ask me questions about my childhood. I froze. *Why was she asking me THAT?*

I didn't see how anything from my past could be affecting my current life. But after a very awkward silence, I gave a condensed version of what I'd been hiding under my mask. This was the second time I'd ever told anyone about the abuse from my dad.

As I shared my past, the therapist pointed out that a lot of my anger seemed to be directed towards my mom. When I stopped to think about it, I realized that I didn't really understand why. Why wasn't I angrier at my dad? Instead, for years now I'd been able to repress the memories of his abuse and "normalize" our relationship.

The therapist explained that part of the stress I felt was probably a result of my past and that I was suffering from Post-Traumatic Stress Disorder (PTSD). She went on to explain that we would need to work together to get to the bottom of it all.

Though I took her card and said thank you, I never called that therapist again. I simply did not feel I had the time or energy to go back to that part of my life. That door was locked. I knew PTSD was a term that is used in relation to the military, but later learned that it can be applied to survivors of any trauma, including sexual abuse and violence.

In time I did a little research and learned that the therapist was correct. According to RAINN (Rape, Abuse and Incest National Network), there are three types of symptoms that indicate PTSD in relation to sexual abuse: hyper-arousal, re-experiencing, and avoidance. My avoidance of the events that had occurred with my parents was making it difficult for me to function in my everyday life.

As my first three sons got a little older, I found that I couldn't let go of my negative feeling towards my parents. I was determined not to let my past get in the way of my future, so instead of trying to work on my emotional issues, I decided I needed something else to do. I began volunteering at our Catholic church as a religious education teacher once a week as well as in my oldest son's elementary school. I found that I really enjoyed it. By this point I had been at home raising kids for eight years and was ready for a new challenge.

I also decided that I wanted to be a teacher, so I went back to school part-time for a Masters in Special Education. I enjoyed my classes, especially because they allowed me to get out twice a week with other people who didn't know me primarily as a mom. I worked hard, looking forward to being a teacher in the future. The course of studies did take me longer than the typical student, since I took two semesters off for the birth of our fourth son.

During these years, I continued to talk on the phone with my parents as well as send them Christmas gifts, birthday gifts, etc. I didn't want to, but the thought of cutting them out of our lives completely left me feeling guilty. On the other hand, pretending to be a loving daughter made me feel like a fake.

My dad in turn sent lots of gifts to the boys. But this too made me angry as I felt he was trying to buy a relationship with them. On a business trip to Washington D.C., he came for another visit and tried to be a fun grandpa. The boys loved him, but John's response to his presence was that of a stone wall, and I was visibly uncomfortable with him being in our house with our kids. I breathed a sigh of relief when he left.

Not long after that, my dad found himself in financial difficulties and had to file for bankruptcy. As a result, he and my mother ended up moving to California to live with my grandparents, Mimi and Fred, until he could find a new job. My dad called regularly to tell me all his woes. I, in turn, felt guilty for not really caring. He'd update me on my mom's drinking and how awful their life together was.

Furiously, I would shout at him, "Then why are you buying her the alcohol?"

My dad would always turn the conversation around so that he was the victim. "If I don't buy it, your mom makes my life a living hell!"

"I don't know how I can help you," I responded. Once we hung up, I would say to myself that I didn't care. But then I wouldn't be able to sleep for the next two days.

What if…? I started asking myself. *What if he died? What if she died? What if they both died together? What would I do? How would*

I know anything about their finances? What would I do with all their belongings?

Eventually I started asking my dad for some of this information and questions about their future. But he would always tell me not to worry, that he'd live forever.

During this entire period, I was filled with fear and worry. I had no idea what the future might hold for my parents and me. I talked to John about my concerns, but he had so many negative feelings towards my dad that it was hard for him to be spiritual about the situation. I was exhausted from spending so much time and effort trying to forget and move on that I became angry. I started to really pray and ask for guidance. But for many years I felt completely alone.

This was a time period when my sense of faith was severely tested. I felt angry at God for letting me go through so many trials with my parents. I wondered if He even cared anymore. I was living wrapped up in my own tight cocoon and wasn't really pursuing a personal relationship with Jesus. At this point I almost felt like giving up on searching after God.

In the Bible, the apostle James talks about this: "You know that under pressure, your faith-life is forced into the open and shows its true colors. So don't try to get out of anything prematurely. Let it do its work so you become mature and well-developed, not deficient in any way." (James 1:3-4, MSG)

When we feel alone in our struggles, we often don't recognize that God is watching over us, keeping an eye on us. We need to remember that even when we can't see or feel Him, God is there. This is faith!

CHAPTER TWELVE

For the next few years, my dad rented an apartment in California while doing contract work for a government agency dealing with encryption. In time, he was able to dig his way out of debt. His job allowed him to work from home, which was a good thing since my mom's health and drinking was getting progressively worse. But my dad wanted to get out of California, so after doing some investigation, he eventually bought a piece of property in Colorado.

My parents rented a house near the property, and my dad began planning their "dream house" to be built on the property. He called me to go over the plans and all the details of the large house he was designing. Considering his previously precarious financial situation, I thought this was ridiculous and completely irresponsible, especially since he was now sixty-five and would soon be retired without a regular salary. But I kept my mouth shut. Since we lived thousands of miles away in Virginia, I felt like I had little control over the situation.

In April, 2002, my dad's father, Fred, who had been gradually declining in health, passed away. I felt so sad for my grandmother, Mimi. They had been married for sixty-two years. I tried to imagine what it would be like to suddenly not have that constant companion in your life. The timing of Fred's funeral made it impossible for me to leave my own family on such short notice.

But I took it upon myself to fly out to visit Mimi in California the following summer. By now she was ninety-five years old.

I was looking forward to having time alone with my grandmother, and since my parents could easily drive from Colorado to California, I deliberately didn't tell them I was going to visit her. Apparently Mimi said something to them about my plans because my dad called me to say he was really hurt that I hadn't told them I was planning to go. I don't remember what I replied, but I was very disappointed when they showed up in California.

Still, I had a wonderful visit with my grandmother and enjoyed spending quality time with her. My dad sat and worked on his laptop almost the entire time, which was fine with me. My mom didn't say much, but exhibited a negative attitude during the whole visit. I didn't let either of these things bother me. I was there to visit Mimi, especially since I didn't know if I would see her ever again. Although at ninety-five she was totally independent and amazingly healthy, I knew she would not live forever.

Mimi and I talked together about my grandfather, and she told me stories about their life together. She showed me photos of them as a couple that I had never seen before. We also talked about God. When I reminded Mimi of our conversation when I was a child about how God answers prayer, she began to cry. In privacy, she shared her concerns about my father's finances and my mother's health. She said that my dad had told her he didn't know what had happened to my relationship with him and didn't understand why I was so distant. I was furious that he was casting the blame on me, but bit my tongue.

The two-bedroom apartment where Mimi now lived was like a small museum. My grandparents had traveled a lot, and over those years of travel she had collected many fine things. She asked me to make a list of items I'd like to have. This made me uncomfortable, but she was firm.

"No one lives forever," she told me.

So I made a small list of jewelry, some furniture, photographs, and trinkets. I starred one particular item on the list: Princess. Mimi had received Princess, a beautiful bisque faced doll, at the age of two from her uncle. Her mother had realized that Mimi was too young for the fragile doll, so for the next three years, Princess went off to boarding school. On Mimi's fifth birthday, Princess returned from boarding school with a trunk containing a new wardrobe of doll clothes. She had been with my grandmother for nearly her whole life and was very special to Mimi. So I really wanted Princess as a remembrance of my grandmother.

By the following summer, Mimi could no longer live alone and was moved into nursing care. About this same time, my dad gave up on the idea of building his dream house on the Colorado property. Instead, he bought a house looking out on the beautiful mountains in the ski area of Taos, New Mexico.

Feeling overwhelmed with the task of taking my mom to California and packing up all my grandparents' belongings, my dad called to ask if I would be able to go to California to help. As much as I wanted to help my grandmother, I was secretly happy that John and I already had plans to go to Italy, which made it impossible for me to go. So my dad and uncle went on alone to pack up the apartment where she and my grandfather had lived.

When John and I returned from our trip, I found a large package waiting for me. My uncle had shipped me a box containing four hand-painted plates originally commissioned for Marie Antoinette. I had seen these plates displayed on my grandparents' living-room wall, but they were not on the wish list I had made for Mimi.

Calling my dad, I asked him about the rest of Mimi's belongings. He explained that he and my uncle had made an agreement. My dad would get any stocks my grandparents held. My uncle got all the belongings. Once my grandmother passed away, the two of them would split any remaining money.

I was stunned. What about my list? My dad told me he knew nothing about it. I then called my uncle to ask about this arrangement the two men had made. My uncle explained that my dad had said he needed the money, not stuff. So Mimi's belongings were all his now. I asked if he had seen my list. He snorted and laughed. "Yes, I saw it."

I reminded my uncle that I had visited Mimi and that she had asked me to make the list. He simply answered that Mimi wanted me to have the plates and that they were quite valuable, so that is what he had sent. I then asked if I could trade the plates and just have Princess. My uncle refused, reminding me that I had gone on vacation while they were doing all the hard work. My aunt—his wife and not even a blood relation to Mimi—was more deserving of Mimi's things, he went on to add.

That is when I raised my voice and started crying. I explained how Mimi was a very important part of my life. He responded unsympathetically, "Yes, we all know you were her favorite grandchild!"

At that I became furious and started raising my voice again. He informed me that I was out of line. I finally just hung up the phone. I never spoke to my uncle again since he passed away from Non-Hodgkin's Lymphoma just a few months later. Nor did I ever get the doll.

Mimi died two years later. Due to a big snowstorm that hit the East Coast, I was not able to fly out to attend her funeral in California. I was deeply saddened by her death. But I can look back now and recognize that my relationship with Mimi was part of what God had given me to help me survive. I love this verse from Ephesians 2:7-9: "For it is by grace you have been saved, through faith… and this is not from yourselves, it is the gift of God." (NLT)

God made sure that I had at least one woman in my life to demonstrate His love to me and to allow me to feel hope. Mimi was a gift to me from God.

CHAPTER THIRTEEN

In August, 2004, John and I celebrated our tenth wedding anniversary. Just a few months later, our fourth son, Jack, was born. By now life had become much easier. We'd moved into a larger house in a beautiful neighborhood in the same general area as we'd been living. John was settled into a new law firm in Washington D.C. Since the other three boys were in school or preschool, I was able to really enjoy special time with this baby.

I was still determined to provide our family with a foundation of faith and an understanding of God's love and the sacrifice of Christ's death on our behalf on the cross. Even though we tried our hardest to go to church every Sunday, it was a challenge. The Catholic church we were then attending expected children to sit still and quiet for an entire hour during the Mass, not an easy task for our crew. I found myself wanting to challenge the priest, inwardly telling him, *you sit here with my four boys, and I'll stand up there and talk to the congregation.*

Sunday mornings became a constant battle to get everyone up, dressed and out the door to church. Once Mass was over and we were back in the car, I'd ask the boys what they'd learned. One day as I was explaining that morning's homily, John looked over at me and interjected, "That's not what it was about."

I felt angry and bitter that I'd clearly missed part of the homily while I was passing out Cheerios, coloring books, and sippy cups.

We finally decided that God would understand if we didn't go to church every Sunday. But it made me sad that I'd come so far and was now going to quit. It didn't seem fair. I desperately wanted to come out of my spiritual cocoon, so much that I started thinking about maybe trying a different church. John didn't like that idea; after all, he'd been raised in the Catholic church. We ended up telling our boys that church was closed for the summer. Instead we filled our Sunday mornings with trips to Home Depot or the grocery store. But I felt like a total hypocrite sending my older sons to Catholic religious education classes, one of which I taught, without attending church myself. I began to wonder just why this seemed so hard for our family.

Summer ended, and that very next fall of 2008, our youngest son began preschool at a newly constructed church called New Hope that was right up the road from our home. Our family took a tour of the facility. My first thought was, *THIS is a CHURCH?*

A large fellowship area held comfortable couches, a fireplace, soda fountains and coffee! The preschool had an indoor playground. The staff was amazing. That Christmas, the children attending their preschool received an invitation to attend a children's Christmas service at the church. I was up for it, but John was a little hesitant. Still, we hadn't been back to our local Catholic church, so I argued that attending this service would at least be better than what we were currently doing. The boys seemed interested in the invitation, so we went.

The moment we stepped into the church building, we were surrounded by people welcoming us. I recognized some other moms from Jack's preschool. Filing into the large auditorium that was the church sanctuary, we sat together as a family in the second row. To my surprise, our four boys didn't squirm during entire service. I was shocked! The boys clearly loved the program while I loved the Christian music. Filled with kind, welcoming people, it felt like home. As we drove out of the parking lot, I looked at the sign and said aloud, "New Hope." Little did I know then what a life changing event that evening would be for our family.

Shortly after our first visit, we began attending New Hope Church regularly, and it transformed our lives in many ways. Our boys loved going to the children's classes on Sunday mornings. John and I enjoyed worshipping together in a way we never had before. This was the point in my life when I truly began to understand what it meant to be a Christian and to rely on Jesus. As John and I met other church members, we made new friends. Within a few months, we had both joined small groups and were attending special church events.

If to this point I had been in the chrysalis phase of my spiritual metamorphosis, I had now finally emerged from the tight, dark space that had trapped me for so long to find myself transformed into a new creature. For the first time in my life, I felt that I had a true connection and relationship with Jesus Christ. I realized that in all my previous searching, I had really only scratched the surface. I formed a group of friends at church who were excited to bring me alongside and help me mature spiritually. My new butterfly wings were still wet and creased at first, but as John and I started reading the Bible together, we both fully accepted and understood what it meant to believe that Jesus Christ is our Savior. I had finally completed my metamorphosis and begun to fly!

CHAPTER FOURTEEN

About the same time my youngest son started preschool and we began attending New Hope Church, I finally received my Master's degree in Special Education and began teaching history classes full time at a public high school. This choice of occupation has worked out nicely for me and for my family since it allows me to work the same schedule as our sons' school calendar.

Several years later, when our oldest son entered middle school and began participating in the church youth group, I began volunteering with the youth group. A few months later, I was invited to become a leader. I have now been working with the youth group for four years. I love seeing the students grow to know and love God and at times feel almost jealous that they have something I didn't even know about until I was an adult.

I have also had the opportunity to accompany teams from the youth group on two mission trips to Guatemala. On these trips, I witnessed God's love shining in even the poorest areas. During our first trip, our group worked with an organization called Clubhouse Guatemala which had a church in an underprivileged neighborhood of Guatemala City. The locals who came to the church relied on the pastor and other volunteers for many resources, including food, clothing, and medical care.

Many teens also congregated at the church as this was their safe place in a city where gangs and crime were the norm. We met neighborhood families and played with the children. On Sunday, we sat in amazement through an entire four hours of church service, joining in with the Guatemalan congregation as they worshipped and prayed. During our week there, we helped run a Vacation Bible School that the church provided for neighborhood children when school was out of session. The youth group team from our church in Virginia did an amazing job with the VBS children and formed friendships with the older kids at the church as well.

On our last night in Guatemala, we leaders realized that our team budget still contained some unused funds. We asked our youth team how they would like to use it. The group voted unanimously to give it to the church to help a teen named Christopher. Our own teenagers had met Christopher at the church. We'd learned that the boy had been kicked out of his own home and was not only homeless, but destitute of any clothing beyond what he wore, not to mention toiletries and other basic necessities. To supplement the money, the boys from our group put together enough of their own toiletries and clothing to fill a small bag for Christopher.

The Guatemalan pastor who was our host showed visible emotion as the translator explained our group's concern for Christopher and desire to help him. When we were saying our goodbyes, I witnessed a fresh outpouring of God's love as my oldest son Bennett removed the shirt off his back to give it to Christopher. The entire week had been a wonderful experience, and it was difficult to leave behind our new church family in Guatemala as we boarded a plane to return home.

The following year, I had the opportunity to return to Guatemala as a chaperone for another youth group mission team, which this time included my second son Charlie. This experience was very different from the first since this time Clubhouse Guatemala had us helping out in a very rural part of Guatemala. The poverty was much worse than what we had experienced in the city, and it was difficult to understand how the people survived in such harsh conditions. We brought baskets of supplies and food to families who lived in lean-tos made of corrugated metal and plastic. Our own youth group team was amazed that the people around us had no electricity, no cars, and no running water.

The entire trip proved a life-changing experience for our American teenagers as they helped build stoves for local families so that they no longer had to cook over an open fire and ingest dangerous fumes. The village children quickly became our friends and wanted to play with us. As we visited with individual families, we would ask if we could pray for them. When we asked this of one family in particular, I saw tears begin rolling down the mother's face. I began to cry as well. I had assumed the mother was going to ask us to pray that she might be able to provide a better life for her children. Instead, our translator told us that she was thanking God for sending us to her.

The mother went on to explain that they had run out of food and she hadn't known how she was going to feed her family that evening. She knew without a doubt that God had heard her prayers and had sent us to her that day. This entire experience was an incredibly moving one for all of us.

During our time there, we also set up crafts, sang songs with the children, and invited the older teens to play soccer with us. Our own teenagers were very humbled on a particular day when our team distributed shoes to the local villagers. The younger children acted giddy with excitement as they tried on several pairs to find one of the right size. As we helped size and pass out shoes, our team couldn't help noticing that the older teens had also lined up, anxiously hoping to receive a pair of shoes as well. Many of these teens were barefoot or wore shoes so worn the soles had holes and their dirty feet were visible through rips in the fabric.

Once we'd distributed all the shoes, we held a celebration. As everyone sang and danced, I noticed that one girl, about 13 years old, hadn't received any shoes. As I looked at her feet and then at my own, I realized our feet were about the same size. Motioning to the girl, I asked her if she'd like to try on the pink Nikes I was wearing.

The girl's face lit up as I slipped off a shoe and handed it to her. It fit perfectly. Later as I walked in my socks back to the local Clubhouse Guatemala dormitory where we were staying, I couldn't stop smiling. On our last morning as I looked around at the filth and poverty of this rural Guatemalan community, I found myself humbled by the faith that I had witnessed among these people living in a part of the world so different and distant from the comfortable lives we knew back in the United States.

Eight years have passed since I first began teaching special education. My own sons Bennett, Charlie, and Will are now among the many teenagers I see walking the halls at my school. I love my job and know this was part of God's plan for me.

Teaching is not my only role at school. When my oldest son Bennett was a sophomore in high school, he and some other students who were friends from the New Hope youth group approached me one day to ask if I would be the faculty sponsor for our school's chapter of Fellowship of Christian Athletes.

I accepted their request and have enjoyed being the leader of a group of such amazing students who meet weekly and have made an impact on the school and in the local community. For example, these students organized a school wide book drive to benefit a local non-profit agency that serves many poor families in our area. The FCA chapter was able to rally support among the student body, and the entire school was filled with pride as we were able to donate over 20,000 books to that non-profit agency.

I remain amazed at what God has done in my life and in my family's life. Who would have guessed that an unchurched, abused, tomboy-looking little girl could end up a leader for young Christians? I had been seeking for God my entire life, and there He was the whole time, just as the Scripture states in Jeremiah

29:13: "You will seek me and find me when you seek me with all your heart."

This verse is a perfect example of God's love at work and speaks volumes about the power of prayer and faith. We all have many burdens, and it is easy to give up when we are going through a difficult time in our life. God knows this, and that is why He sent Jesus to us. We will never be able to be as perfect as Jesus, but if we lean on Him and try to follow His example, our faith will allow us to know Him better.

CHAPTER FIFTEEN

Looking back over the years, I am so thankful for the constant presence John's parents have been in my sons' lives. They have come to as many of the boys' sporting and school events as they can. They are always quick to tell our sons, "Great job!"

It was to be expected that when our sons were old enough to notice the difference, they would begin asking questions about their other grandparents and why we never saw them. For a while it was easy to make excuses. They lived too far away. Traveling to see them was too expensive.

But as our older sons got to be teenagers, and we began taking more extensive vacations ourselves, it became evident to them that our excuses were just that—excuses. I felt guilty as I realized my sons just wanted to know their other grandparents. After all, they didn't have any cousins or other extended family.

I finally told our three oldest sons that my parents hadn't shown me love as a child and that the way they had treated me still hurt me even now as an adult. I explained that I didn't want my parents to have an opportunity to hurt them as they had hurt me. I was worried that my explanation sounded selfish, but the boys accepted it readily enough. I also felt pressure from John's parents as they would often ask when I'd last spoken to my parents.

So now we are back to the beginning of this story in the spring of 2013 when I first heard my pastor speaking about forgiveness.

After I had sent the letter to my dad and didn't receive a reply, I made a conscious decision to stop corresponding with my parents. Easter, my oldest son's birthday, and both my parents' birthdays followed. These events became awkward as my dad would call and I would put on my fake act once again. My dad continued to complain about my mom's drinking and her frequent falling down. Their relationship was at an all-time low, and she was depressed and combative with him.

My parents had also moved again, purchasing a large house in Santa Fe, New Mexico. The house in Taos had been rented out. I continued to resent the fact that my dad still felt he could dump his problems on me, and every phone call left me with mixed emotions. First I'd feel guilty that I couldn't help. Then I'd feel angry that I cared. These feelings would go back and forth in my mind until I found myself turning to a glass of wine with a friend to make it all go away.

During July, 2013, just four months after my pastor had preached on forgiveness, John and I rented a house on the beach in the Outer Banks of North Carolina for a week of fun with our boys. We'd invited John's parents to join us, and one afternoon during our time there, John's mom and I went on a walk together along the beach. As we walked, she asked me what I heard from my parents.

At her question, I felt a tug at my heart. John and I had been married for nineteen years at this point, and I realized it was time for me to tell his parents the truth. As my mother-in-law and I walked together through the sand, I told her the whole story. I was scared that she would judge me or blame me, and I didn't want to jeopardize our relationship. I was relieved when she stopped and gave me a big hug. Instead of judging me, she told me that she loved me and was sorry for all I had been through. We continued to cry and talk as we walked along the beach, the surf washing up over our feet.

Later that evening I told John about my walk with his mother, and he asked why I had decided to tell her. I told him that I couldn't explain it; I just felt like I needed to. He didn't say anything more, but I think he felt as relieved as I did to have his parents finally know the truth.

After years of arthritis and other health problems, my dad had been scheduled for a knee replacement surgery in September, 2013. He called me to say that he was thinking about what he should do with my mom while he was recovering. Not for the first time, I suggested that my mom needed to be in an assisted living facility where she could interact with other people and receive physical therapy. If he found a facility where they could both stay during his own recuperation, then perhaps she could stay on once he was healed.

Then in August, 2013, just weeks before the scheduled knee surgery, my dad fell and broke his lower leg. Surgery was necessary to insert pins and a metal plate that would hold the bones back in their proper place. Once my dad was released from the hospital, he was still confined to a wheelchair, which made it very difficult for him to take care of both their house and my mom. At my insistence, my parents moved into an assisted living facility for what they thought would be about a month until my dad could get back on his feet again. But just a few weeks later, right before Labor Day, my dad called again to let me know he had to go back in for surgery because the incision had become infected.

Labor Day activities marked the unofficial end of the summer, after which the school year began. During my first week back in the classroom, I received a call from a man I didn't know. He introduced himself as a "friend of my parents". He asked me if I knew that my dad was in the hospital.

Still? I'd thought this second surgery was just going to be a quick in and out. *Where was my mom?* My world started spinning out of control as I tried to understand what was going on. The caller gave me the name of the hospital and a phone number for my mom.

When I called the hospital in New Mexico, I found out that my dad had developed a systemic infection from the surgery. He'd then developed pneumonia and had to be intubated. The doctor was very concerned and asked if my dad had a Do Not Resuscitate (DNR) order. I had no idea. I called my mom and found her extremely distraught. At the time my dad had gone back into the hospital, they had only been in the assisted living facility about a week, and she had no idea what was going on.

I explained what I had learned from the hospital and told her that the doctor had asked me about a DNR. She told me my dad didn't have one, so I asked her what measures he would want. At this point we both thought he would pull through, so we agreed that the hospital could perform life-saving measures if necessary.

For the next two days, I was in touch with the hospital and my mom while juggling work and the start to my boys' fall sports season. I learned that the "friend" of my parents was actually a handyman who'd been staying at my parent's house while they were at the assisted living facility. This friend, Steve, began calling me regularly. He told me he'd visited my mom and had taken her to the hospital to see my dad.

At first I was thankful for this man's kindness and friendship to my parents. But the more I spoke to him, the more suspicious I became of his intentions. At this point I had no idea what was going to happen to my dad. I explained to Steve what the doctor had told me and suggested he find another living arrangement as I didn't know what the future would look like for my parents (and to be honest, I was tired of dealing with the man!).

The truth came out when Steve informed me that my dad owed him $30,000 and that he had nowhere to go. I told Steve that I had no control over my parents' money and could do nothing for him. Steve suggested he could have my mom write him a check, then take it to the bank. Suddenly I realized that this "friend" was a snake.

Getting on the phone with Steve, my husband threatened to call the police if Steve didn't leave my parents' house. Steve then insisted he didn't have a driver's license, family, or any money. We reiterated our ultimatum and told Steve he needed to vacate the house immediately. I then called my mom to tell her that I didn't trust Steve and that she was to give him nothing. My mom sounded confused and insisted my dad didn't owe Steve that much money.

After the conversation with my mom, I immediately contacted a lawyer in New Mexico and explained my situation. The lawyer suggested I get a conservatorship that would permit me to assist my mom with finances. He went on to explain that if my dad passed away, I could also become my mother's legal guardian.

Over the next few days, my head was spinning non-stop. The doctors called to tell me that my dad had a fever and wasn't responding to the antibiotics. They had tried twice to take my dad off life support, but both attempts had failed. When I asked what his options were, the doctor explained that if my dad wasn't able to breathe on his own, he would need a tracheotomy. I asked if this would be permanent and if he'd be able to talk. The doctor couldn't give me any definite answers. Instead, they encouraged me to fly to New Mexico to see my father's condition for myself and make some decisions.

By this time I felt like I was watching an episode of The Twilight Zone. My worst fear was about to come true. Going in to work, I explained to my school administrator that I would need to take some time off from teaching. I leaned on my friends for support and tried to hold on to a Bible verse that had come to mean a lot to me: "I can do all things through him who gives me strength." (Philippians 4:13, NLT)

CHAPTER SIXTEEN

My father now lay in the hospital, unresponsive to antibiotics. My mother remained confused and scared in an assisted living facility. Meanwhile, my husband John was preparing for a trial at his law firm and couldn't leave work. So I was thankful when my mother-in-law kindheartedly offered to go to New Mexico with me. I am convinced now it was the Holy Spirit who gave me the courage just a few weeks prior to this crisis to share my past with John's mom as we walked on that beach.

When our plane flight landed in New Mexico, I turned on my phone to see that I had several missed calls and a voicemail message. When I listened to the first message, it was from the assisted living facility, informing me that a man (Steve the snake!) had called to tell them he was going to take my mom home.

My heart started racing in a panic. Was Steve going to kidnap my mom for ransom? I called the assisted facility back immediately, instructing them not to release my mom to anyone and that I didn't want Steve to be able to see her. I tried to call Steve, but he didn't answer.

The next message was from the hospital, alerting me that my dad's doctor was at the hospital and would wait to meet with me. My mother-in-law and I had planned to go see my mom first, but after hearing the message from the hospital, we took a cab straight from the airport to the hospital.

There I met with my dad's doctors. I'd expected to discuss the options we had discussed on the phone, including the possibility of a tracheotomy. Knowing that my dad wouldn't want to be hooked up to life support machines for the rest of his life, I had lots of questions as to what that might involve. The doctor asked me to hold on to my questions. He went on to tell me that they had done a test to see if the infection had gone to my dad's heart. If so, there would be no other option than surgery. However, after having spent the last fourteen days on life support, my dad would not survive such an operation. The doctor suggested I visit with my dad while we waited for the results to come back.

Since my father had an infection, we had to wear gloves and a gown to approach him. As I walked towards the ICU bay where he was being cared for, I didn't even recognize the man lying on the bed. He looked small, frail and old. Seven different tubes were connected to his body. A ventilator was forcing him to breathe, and I felt my own lungs breathing in rhythm with the machine. Standing there awkwardly, I didn't know what to do. Could my dad hear me? What should I say?

Eventually a nurse came in. She informed us that someone from the assisted living facility had brought my mom to see my dad earlier that day. In a weak voice, I finally said, "Hi, Dad, it's me. Can you hear me?"

He made no response. As I looked at the tubes connecting my dad to life support apparatus and listened to the various noises the machines made, I suddenly felt sick. I couldn't stay in that room any longer. John's mom and I excused ourselves, and I walked down the hallway toward the elevators to catch my breath. Near the elevators, some green plastic chairs offered seating for family members and other visitors. As my mother-in-law sat in one chair and I in another, I began to pray silently.

Dear Heavenly Father, I need You more than ever right now. Please help me. I am scared that I will have to make a decision regarding my father's life, and I really don't want to do that. Please, God, help the doctors get the necessary information so that the path I need to take will be clear. Please, please, please, God, I can't do this without You. You've gotten me this far, and I know You love me, so I'm begging you...

Just a few minutes later, the nurse came to summon my mother-in-law and I back to my father's ICU bay. As soon as we entered, I saw three other hospital personnel standing around my dad. I knew it couldn't be good. Once the nurse slid shut the door to the bay, the doctor explained to us that the test showed my father's infection had reached his aortic valve.

By now my hands were sweating in the rubber gloves I'd had to put on to enter the ICU. I felt as though I couldn't breathe. Someone was saying something about hospice. But my head was whirling, and I could see stars. Gasping for air, I asked if I could sit down.

At this point someone whisked me out of the bay and gave me water. Once I could breathe normally, John's mom made sure I understood what was happening. "Your dad has an infection in his heart. The only way to get rid of it is with surgery, which he won't survive. All they can do is make him comfortable, remove the tubes, and let him go peacefully."

I nodded my consent. Then we collected my dad's personal belongings. After I signed some papers, we headed to the elevators. As we stepped into the elevator and the doors began to close, I looked over towards the green plastic chairs where we'd been sitting earlier, convinced I would see God sitting there. Though I saw nothing, I knew beyond a doubt that He had answered my prayer, lifting from me the burden of making a decision about my father's life.

Once we arrived back down at the hospital lobby of the hospital, my knees felt weak and I had to sit down. I needed a little time to comprehend what had just happened. I wasn't sure how I was supposed to feel. I felt some sadness, but mostly relief and confirmation that God had heard my prayer. Later that afternoon, on Friday, September 13, 2013, exactly six months after my pastor had delivered the message about forgiveness, my father passed away.

Chapter Seventeen

The drive from the hospital to the assisted living facility passed by in a blur. I couldn't believe what had just happened. As I watched the landscape outside the cab window roll by, I quietly thanked God for helping me and asked Him to keep watching and guiding me in the coming days as I approached many unknowns. One comforting verse came to my mind: *"God promises to make good out of the storms that bring devastation to your life."* (Romans 8:26)

My heart was feeling heavy by the time my mother-in-law and I arrived at the assisted living center. I hadn't seen my mom in several years and was nervous about our reunion. To my relief, I found her to be in good health and SOBER. She walked quite slowly and required a walker for balance, but overall seemed pretty healthy except for her smoking.

My mom in turn hadn't seen my mother-in-law since my wedding, so the two women settled down to chat about their grandsons. As I looked around the apartment, I saw some of my father's things. I said to myself: *This is it! This is the moment I've been worried about.*

I knew that my next step was simply to figure out what I was going to do. First, I introduced myself to the assisted living facility staff. They all sounded shocked to hear about my dad. The staff were very helpful, filling me in on my mom's medications and level of care. My mom seemed to be in good spirits and so happy to see us that I didn't tell her about my dad's condition until that evening when I received notice from the hospital that he had passed away.

When she heard the news, my mom collapsed into tears. She had never been an emotional person, so watching her sobs was very difficult for me. But after all, despite their problems, my parents had been married just shy of forty-five years. As with my grandmother Mimi, my mom was now without the partner who had been part of her life all these years. Looking up at me, my mom wailed, "What am I going to do?"

I promised my mom that I would be there to help her. Together we would figure things out. But I really had no idea where to begin, so I started making lists. I contacted the lawyer I'd spoken to on the phone earlier in the week. He proved very helpful at getting all the paperwork in place so that I could receive temporary guardianship and a financial conservatorship for my mom.

I had no idea how much money my parents had or owed. I had a bad feeling about this because my dad had moved around chasing the next big thing for the past twenty years. I knew he had declared bankruptcy at one point and had borrowed a lot of money from my grandparents. I was hopeful he hadn't spent all the money he'd received after Mimi had died. I kept trying to call "the friend" (Steve the snake). But he had turned off his phone.

Trying to get some information from my mom, I finally asked, "What is the name of the bank you and dad use?"

"Oh, let me think," she replied. "It's the one with the big statue of Pocahontas in front."

I wasn't sure if I should laugh or cry at her response. Looking through all the papers on my dad's desk at the assisted living facility, I did find a checkbook. This was at least a start. I had received his wallet from the hospital. From the ATM and other cards I found inside, I was able to piece together few clues. It felt like trying to put together a crime scene. I had never been to the house where my parents lived in Santa Fe or the one they were renting in Taos. After briefly assessing the financial situation, I realized that for my mom to continue living with assistance, it would be necessary to sell both houses.

I called my late uncle's wife to tell her what had happened. She was kind and offered advice, having gone through my uncle's death not too long before. I told her I had nothing to work with—no will, no plan. Nothing was in order. My aunt told me she'd discussed the future with my dad and encouraged him to make plans while he was healthy, just in case. She had even offered to have my parents move in with her in Florida to give my dad some help with my mom. Hearing this left me frustrated and angry.

The next few days were full of new experiences. My mother-in-law and I managed to rent a room at the assisted living facility where my mom was. The staff was amazingly helpful. Rather than rent a car, we decided to use my dad's car. This was not just your average car. It was a big FJ Cruiser, equivalent to a small tank on giant wheels. I started laughing as I walked around the vehicle. It had a winch on the front, ladder on the back, and every extra available.

As I drove the Cruiser through town towards the bank the next day, John's mom and I were laughing at how ridiculous two small women must look in such a massive car. To my surprise, as we parked the Cruiser to head into the bank, several people commented on how much they liked the car. We were walking into the bank when I stopped on the sidewalk and started laughing.

"What?" John's mom demanded.

I was laughing so hard I couldn't reply. I just pointed. There in front of us stood a large statue of Pocahontas, just as my mom had said.

After spending an hour with the bank manager, I had a better handle on my parent's accounts and felt I was making progress. We drove back to the assisted living facility. Before getting out of the Cruiser, we decided to look through it for more clues. Seeing my father's personal items—sunglasses, nail clippers, gum—was unsettling.

Then my mother-in-law opened the glove box. We both froze. Lying on top of some papers was a gun. All this time we'd been driving around with it and we didn't have a gun license, I realized. In fact, I'd never even *held* a gun before.

Panicking, I called my husband. He told me to take the gun out of the car in case we got pulled over. Reaching into the glove box, I carefully pulled it out by the handle. Together my mother-in-law and I placed it in a bag, then gingerly carried it to our room as though it were a poisonous snake. Once we got it to the room, we laid the gun on the floor, then stared at it. Only then did I notice it was cocked and there was a bullet in the chamber (I'd learned that much from watching cop shows). Now what?

My mother-in-law and I agreed neither of us would be able to sleep knowing the gun was in our room. So we decided to take it back to the car for the night. We very carefully slipped the gun back into the bag, then snuck it back down to the car. By the time we slipped back to our room like a pair of thieves in the night, both of us were doubled over in laughter.

This whole experience had been surreal since my mother-in-law and I had stepped off the airplane, and it didn't stop there. The next morning we called the police and explained the situation. They sent an officer over to help out. After he unloaded it for us (silly East Coast women!), we were able to breathe a sigh of relief. I later learned that everyone in New Mexico carries a gun and that having one in the car was very normal.

But despite the humor and laughter of the gun incident, I was feeling like a robot as I worked my way down the list I'd made. First I met with a funeral director the hospital had suggested and explained there would not actually be a funeral.

"So where would you like the body to be buried?" the funeral director asked me.

Looking over at my mother-in-law, I had no idea what to say. When I asked if we could have a minute, the funeral director left the room. Quickly calling my mom, I asked her what she wanted to do. The two of us agreed he should be cremated, but then what? My mom remembered that my uncle had been buried in St. Louis next to my grandparents. She thought doing the same for my father would be a good idea.

My next call was to my aunt for information on my uncle's burial. The next day I met with a New Mexico state social worker who was representing my mom. Thirty minutes after finishing with the social worker, I met with the lawyer. I was so thankful my mother-in-law was with me because my brain was not fully functioning. I was facing options and questions I'd never even considered before and felt very overwhelmed.

After the lawyer, my mother-in-law and I went to the local post office to have my parents' mail forwarded to my address in Virginia. I then contacted a realtor in Taos to list the house my parents owned there and were renting out. As we continued down the list, we took time each evening to have dinner with my mom. I was enjoying the time with her and could tell she was relieved to have us there.

The next step involved my mother-in-law and I driving to Santa Fe to see the house where my parents had actually been living until a few weeks past when my father broke his leg.

The houses in the area they lived were adobe-style, something I wasn't used to seeing, having grown up on the East Coast. The surrounding landscape was desert-brown with lots of cacti and very few trees.

My parents' own home was a large and rambling one-story house with a circular driveway and a small patio at the entrance. The entire front and back of the house had large windows to show off amazing views of nearby mountains. I'd been nervous that "the friend" Steve might still be squatting in the house, so we had asked a police officer to meet us there. But when the officer checked the house, no one was there. Going inside, I found to my relief no evidence that anything had been stolen.

As I looked around, I was comforted to see some things I remembered from my youth. I immediately recognized a large, wood coffee table, my mom's Lenox swan ashtray, and a picture of Mimi and Fred.

But I also observed many things in the house I'd never seen before. I noticed Native American style woven rugs and wall hangings, an unfamiliar kitchen table and wine rack. As I walked through the rooms and began inventorying the items, I wondered, *what am I going to do with all this stuff?*

Remembering that my father had been in a financial crisis just a few years earlier, I was also appalled by some of what I saw. The house held thousands of dollars of photography equipment, professional cooking equipment, including over a hundred professional quality pots and pans. There was a home theater, a large gun collection, and an office full of electronic equipment.

By the time I'd gone through the house, I felt completely overwhelmed. The "friend" had left dirty dishes in the sink, and the guest quarters where he'd been staying looked and smelled like a fraternity house. Since my parents had assumed they'd be at the assisted living facility for just a short time, they hadn't bothered packing many personal items or clothes. So my mother-in-law and I gathered more of my mom's clothes, some pictures, and a few knick-knacks to take back to my mom.

Fearing that Steve might return, I called a locksmith to come and change all the locks on the house. When we finally returned to the assisted living facility that evening, the manager greeted us and expressed her condolences. She asked me if I thought my mom might like to move to a different apartment. Talking through the idea with my mom, I realized that such a change might help her transition from being with my father. My mom was happy to move into a first floor apartment, which would include a patio where she could smoke. I, in turn, was thrilled with this opportunity to give her a fresh start.

Movers came in to help as we packed up my father's belongings and got my mom settled in her new space. By the end of our week in New Mexico, I felt physically and mentally exhausted. Our last night there, I had a meltdown, no longer able to process or think straight. I had no idea how I was going to manage everything that I still had to do in New Mexico while returning to work full-time and being a good wife and mother. As I prepared to fly home, I felt terrible leaving my newly widowed mom alone.

Thankfully, the facility staff was wonderful, promising to keep an eye on my mom. And I assured her I'd be back in a few weeks with John. Even though my mom and I had been through so much conflict in the past, I suddenly felt the need to care for her. After all, she had only a few friends and no family. I started thinking of having her move to an assisted living facility close to my family in Virginia. I even began visualizing her with my sons at family gatherings, sporting events, church, etc. Could this maybe even be a fresh start for us?

CHAPTER EIGHTEEN

Once I'd returned to Virginia, I felt as though I'd just woken up from a bad dream. Exhausted and depressed, I found myself conflicted about this new feeling of kindness I was having for my mother. I began having flashbacks and would wake up in a cold sweat at night.

As reality set in, I recognized I was not going to be able to work while trying to deal with all these emotions and my new responsibilities. So I took the next three months off from teaching. Instead I spent my days sorting through my parents' mail and trying to fit together the puzzle pieces of their business affairs. Did they have any savings? Mortgages? Pension? Life insurance?

The lawyer in New Mexico proved a tremendous help and was able to obtain for me my parents' taxes from the previous year, which listed all their accounts. I cancelled cable, Wi-Fi, magazine and newspaper subscriptions. I called several different estate sale companies and set up appointments to meet once I returned to New Mexico. My dining room table became covered with file folders as I tried to make sense of this puzzle.

In the midst of everything I was dealing with, I turned to God. I asked Him to help me understand why all of this had happened. I prayed for strength and compassion towards my mother. It was then that I realized there was no way I could just abandon my mom in the middle of a New Mexico desert. So I began making appointments to check out assisted living facilities in our own area.

As I busied myself with the task of obtaining information, I found myself reminiscing and dwelling on the past. To make matters worse, one day I received a phone call from my father's boss. She expressed how devastated she felt by his loss and told me that my father and she had talked on the phone every day. As she went on and on about how wonderful my father was, she commented, "You know, he was very sad that you two were estranged. He said that you hadn't been to visit them for sixteen years!"

As she went on telling me what a great man my father was, I could feel anger, hatred, and self-pity sweeping over me. At that point I realized that I needed to talk to someone. It was time for me to go back for real into the darkness of my past until I was able to turn the light on. This was it, no more hiding!

I went to a female therapist who'd been recommended by a friend. Unfortunately, after three sessions of doing all the talking, I wasn't left with much and didn't feel any better. I knew John still held a lot of anger towards my father and possibly my mother, so I didn't feel comfortable talking to him. However, John and I did begin talking about the possibility of moving my mother to be close to us in Virginia, and he was supportive of the idea.

A few weeks after my mother-in-law and I returned home, John and I went to New Mexico together. There we visited with my mom, met with the lawyer, and then got to work. We went through my parents' house with a fine-toothed comb, looking for personal items and valuables to set aside before we scheduled an estate sale. This was an exhausting three day job. It was emotionally draining to see pictures I'd sent of our babies still in their envelopes, contrasted with a framed certificate from "Jeep Camp" in my dad's office. I was upset to find old, stained clothing in my mom's closet and designer clothes in my dad's.

It quickly became obvious that my dad's priorities revolved around himself, and I wanted to scream. Although I'd always known he was self-centered, this became more concrete as I looked around my parents' house. Standing in my dad's office, a cold sweat came over me. What if I found the letter I had sent? What if he hadn't opened it?

When I verbalized my fear, John suggested he go through the rest of my dad's papers by himself while I went on into another room. We did not find the letter. Over the days, we catalogued everything in the house, making decisions. Do we take the china and the silver? What about family photos? Do we need any more pots or pans?

John and I began laughing and making jokes to eases the tension we both felt. We boxed and wrapped items to be shipped to Virginia. Other items were set aside for my mom. Everything else would be left behind to sell or donate. Standing in that unfamiliar house and seeing knick-knacks from my youth filled me with mixed emotions. I could point to a familiar object and remember where it had been in the Virginia house we'd acquired from Aunt Judy. The large Oriental brass plate had hung over the fireplace. The large wooden pepper grinder that always sat in the middle of the dining room table.

Remembering that childhood home brought up unpleasant feelings, and I suddenly wanted to escape. As we left the Santa Fe house for the last time, I realized I was leaving behind memories of my youth to be sold. Despite the unpleasant feelings they evoked, the finality of abandoning such familiar items left me feeling very conflicted.

John and I spent a few days exploring the area and relaxing a bit before we returned to my mom at the assisted living facility. While there, I began discussing with my mom the idea of moving to Virginia. She was hesitant and didn't know how she could possibly get through the airport and on a plane. She had relied on my dad for everything and nothing. Her movements had always been controlled by his wants, and she'd been left with insecurities about her physical abilities.

It took a lot of convincing, but by the time John and I flew back to Virginia, my mom had agreed to the move. My next trip to New Mexico would be to go to court with my mom in order to become her legal guardian, pack all her belongings, and get her on an airplane. I had only one month to make all that happen. I also needed to figure out what to do about my dad's car. This problem took an interesting turn. While John and I were still visiting my mom in the assisted living facility, I had gone to the lobby, which had a coffee station, to get a cup of coffee.

At the coffee station, I met a man who had a sister in the same facility as my mom. We began talking about the challenges related to having a family member who needed assistance, and I found myself telling him my own circumstances. Shaking my head in disbelief, I explained how my dad had recently passed away. Because I was going to be moving my mom to Virginia, I now needed to sell two houses and my dad's car as soon as possible.

Saying goodbye to my mom this second time around wasn't so difficult as I knew I'd be coming back within a month to take her to Virginia. I was actually getting excited. This was going to be an opportunity to have the relationship with my mom I'd wanted for so long.

Looking out at the clouds from the airplane window as John and I flew back to Virginia, I thought about the last few weeks. I remembered my first flight to New Mexico with John's mom and how I had been so full of confusion and doubt. I was still far from getting everything figured out, but I had a new sense of confidence that I knew could have only come from God. There is another verse I love in the Bible: "Therefore we do not lose heart. Though outwardly we are wasting away, yet inwardly we are being renewed day by day." (2 Corinthians 4:16)

What this Scripture tells us is that even when things look like they are falling apart on the outside, God is working on the inside and filling us with His grace. This was very clear to me at that particular moment!

Chapter Nineteen

Once John and I had returned from New Mexico, I kicked myself into high gear. I found a great retirement community just ten minutes away from our own house. Someone had just vacated an apartment, which the facility could have ready in time for my mom to arrive before Thanksgiving. Calling my mom, I told her all about it, trying to get her as excited as I was becoming. I shopped for items for her new apartment, wanting everything to be just right for her, for us.

The timing was perfect as my mom would arrive right before the holiday season. I pictured us baking Christmas cookies and going shopping together. Looking back, I realize this was not very realistic. But I think I was so desperate for the relationship I'd never had with my mom that I put reality aside.

I arrived in New Mexico for the third time, just two months after my dad had died. I had several items to deal with before taking my mom to Virginia. I needed to figure out what to do about my dad's car. I needed to go before a judge to be officially appointed as my mom's guardian in court. I also needed to sort out what items my mom would want to take with her immediately to Virginia rather than shipping with her furniture and other belongings.

As my cab pulled up to the assisted living center, I noticed a note someone had placed on my dad's car. The note said, "I would like to buy this car if it is for sale."

Someone wanted to buy the car? Thank you, Jesus! I called a phone number included in the note. A man answered. I agreed to meet him in the facility lobby that same afternoon. The man turned out to be the same one I'd met by the coffee pot at the end of my last visit. He wanted the car for his son.

I explained I was only there for a few days and that he and his son would need to get me the money before I left. We agreed on a great selling price and were able to finalize all the details before my mom and I headed back to Virginia. I thanked God as I was sure He had a hand in it all.

The day after the car sale was our court date with the judge over my mom's guardianship. I didn't know what to expect. My mom and I had to be dressed and ready to go early since our court appointment was set for 8:00 AM. My mom is not a morning person, so this was already presenting a challenge. She had known about the early schedule for some time, but continued to complain as we got ready and drove to the courthouse.

Once we arrived, my mom and I met with the lawyer, state appointed guardian, and social worker. The judge was not yet there, so we all waited for him to arrive, then entered the courtroom. It was a surreal experience as the gavel came down, signaling for us to rise to our feet. The lawyer explained why we were there. After my mom and I each answered a few questions, I was appointed to be the guardian and conservator of my mom and her estate.

The whole process proved much easier than I had expected. When we left, I had to laugh as I looked over at my mom and told her, "I'm in charge now!"

My mom and I went out for a big breakfast to celebrate. As we reflected on the previous weeks that had brought us back together, my mom thanked me for everything I had done. I bit my lip, fighting back tears at her words.

Next on the agenda was packing up my mom's belongings at the assisted living facility. Her new apartment at the Virginia living facility would be provided with basic furnishings until her own items arrived on a moving truck. Over the next two days, I helped my mom pick out those items she would want in Virginia right away, and we packed as many of her clothes as possible into suitcases.

By now my mom was visibly distraught. She wanted to pack everything she had in the suitcases. When I tried to explain we couldn't take it all with us on the plane, she snapped at me. For the third, fourth, fifth time, I tried to explain what was going to happen, then just started replying, "Okay."

To prevent my mom from a total meltdown, I sent her to the lobby once the movers arrived to get us some coffee. My mom and I spent that last night together in a guest room at the assisted living center. I felt like I had the first time I'd babysat. What if my mom fell out of her bed or in the shower? What if I forgot to give her the medication the facility staff had released to me? What if there was a fire?

Thankfully, we survived the night with no problems and prepared for our next adventure together—the airport. As we left the facility and headed towards our future together, I texted a friend. She texted me back the following verse:

"Consider it pure joy, my brothers and sisters, whenever you face trials of many kinds, because you know that the testing of your faith produces perseverance. Let perseverance finish its work so that you may be mature and complete, not lacking anything." (James 1:2-4, NIV)

Had she sent this to me any earlier, I would not have been able to appreciate its meaning. After all, who considers trials a joy? But now I can see the joy in that situation. God had tested my faith in a big way, and I had persevered. Life is full of curveballs and unexpected events that can feel like a detour to our own desires. Our faith helps us get through these times and allows us to lean on Him for strength.

CHAPTER TWENTY

My mom and I arrived in Virginia after a remarkably smooth trip through airport security, to the gate, and onto the plane. A wheelchair had been supplied for my mom, and I was very appreciative of the porter who assisted us with it. My mom did great throughout, and I joked with her that I was going to have to start traveling with her more often.

John met us at the airport. As we headed to the retirement center, I was giddy with excitement to show my mom her new apartment. My boys had made a big banner to welcome their grandmother and hung it on her door. Once at the assisted living facility, we met the nurses, got my mom settled, and told her we'd be by the next day. As we drove away, I breathed a huge sigh of relief. The emotional roller coaster of the last few weeks finally felt like it was slowing down.

In time my mom's furniture and other belongings arrived from New Mexico. Today my mom's new apartment in Virginia looks very nice. We have celebrated our first holidays together and are getting used to being in each other's lives. My mom has made a few friends, but doesn't do many of the extra activities at the retirement center. She has refused physical therapy despite my attempts to do it with her, which frustrates me. She is very unsteady without her walker, and I worry she is going to fall and break a hip or something else. With her approval, I got my mom an adult cat to keep her company and give her a sense of responsibility. I visit her or take her out a least three times a month and call her frequently.

So now the relationship with my mom has come full circle. By moving her to Virginia, I had hoped to get what I wanted so badly as a child—hugs, warm pancakes, and love. Our mutual journey hasn't quite ended up there, but I know that I can trust God to keep me safe and loved. There is hope for those of us who put our trust in Jesus. It hasn't always been easy, but this journey of faith has brought me to where I am today, and for that I am thankful.

CHAPTER TWENTY-ONE

So today my mom is once again part of my life. Just as my new relationship with her began to unfold, I was invited to attend a women's retreat. There I heard several wonderful speakers and found myself wrestling with my emotions from the previous months following my father's death. One speaker who was a Christian counselor told a story about her sister who, as the speaker described, had "been to hell and back."

I felt like jumping up and yelling, "I've been there too!"

The speaker talked about how her sister's faith and trust in God helped her get through her tough situation. The speaker went on to give other examples from some of her counseling clients who were or had been struggling to understand why certain circumstances had happened to them. As I listened to this speaker explain how she'd helped these clients lean on their faith to achieve an understanding of their circumstances, I knew I needed to talk to her.

One day during the retreat, I spoke to the counselor privately after lunch. After telling her how much I'd enjoyed her session, I asked if she would have any time to meet with me after the retreat. She replied that she was not currently taking new clients, but would be able to put me on a waiting list.

I wasn't optimistic about her response, but recognized I really needed help to sort out my emotions, so I began praying. I prayed that if I couldn't speak with this particular counselor, God would put someone else in my path who could help me. When the counselor ended up contacting me the very next week, I was pleasantly surprised.

I met with this counselor for several weeks, laying everything about my messy past on the table. She never judged me nor acted shocked as my story unfolded. Through these sessions, I have been able to understand and accept that I am who I am because of my past and all I have had to endure to overcome it.

As we were meeting one afternoon, the counselor commented that she saw me as a shining example of God's grace. She went on to say that I had a story that could help others. Then she asked me if I could ever see myself sharing that story. I began laughing nervously, but couldn't ignore the growing excitement inside of me.

As I left her office and headed to my car, I found myself considering the crazy idea of writing this book. I kept it to myself for a week. Then I received an e-mail invitation from a Christian women's organization called Proverbs 31 Ministries to attend a conference for female writers and speakers called *She Speaks* in Charlotte, North Carolina. I had never received an e-mail from this organization before, and I saw it as a confirmation that this was something God was calling me to do.

I was excited, but scared, and too nervous to tell my husband in person, so I e-mailed him. John is a logical, no-nonsense, lawyer, so I think I was waiting—hoping?—for him to tell me this was a silly idea. Instead, he wrote back, "Go for it!"

John's answer confirmed to me this was not something I could just ignore. I flew to the conference, feeling very nervous and unprepared. I had a skeleton of a book proposal and brand new business cards. Once at the conference, I felt overwhelmed to be in the company of so many incredible speakers and published authors. However, as I began to mingle with other conferees, I was relieved to find myself with a lot of other women who were just starting out like me.

When we first broke into small groups at the conference, I was uncomfortable telling strangers my idea for a book. But I soon found that the more I told people about my idea, the more positive reinforcement I received. As I left the conference, I was sure that God had given me this purpose. I headed home on a mission to write a book!

Shortly after that conference, seven months after my last trip to New Mexico, both of my parents' houses sold in the same month. Thankfully, with the sales of the two houses, my mom will be financially set for the rest of her life. I felt as though I'd done everything in my power to help her. But something was still missing. My "happily ever after" ending had yet to come. I have made so many efforts to suggest activities for my mom or to buy her new things, only to meet with more rejection. With the help of my Christian counselor, I have come to realize that I am not responsible for my mom's happiness.

Today my visions of my mom and me being the mother/daughter team I always wanted are not panning out quite as I had hoped. My mom in general is not a happy person and often complains to me. When I try to talk to her about it, she shuts down.

Still, I visit my mom regularly, and we include her in family gatherings. My sons now know their other grandmother. If our relationship isn't as I hoped, she is at least cordial to my friends and John's parents. Though she isn't interested in outings and activities planned by the retirement community, she does go on the shuttle bus once a week to the grocery store for snacks or other necessities, and has become more cordial towards the other residents over time.

Meanwhile I continue to pray for my mom and hope that in time she will find something to make her happy. We have invited her to our church, which she has politely declined. My ultimate wish for her is that she would open her heart to listen to the word of God and begin a relationship with Him through Jesus.

CHAPTER TWENTY-TWO

So what are the next steps for my own life journey? For one, I have grown so much from this experience, and I know now that I am going to be okay. I still experience feelings of anger and bitterness towards my dad. Some days I feel that he got off easy. Did he ever feel guilty about what he did to me? Was he at all remorseful?

As painful as it is to wrestle with the many unanswered questions, I know too that I have come through all of this only because of God and His immeasurable grace. I am a wiser and richer person because of my past experiences and my growing dependency on God. I have grown in my faith and feel confident about my future. I am able to tell my story without feeling sick. And since I began sharing it with my counselor, my small group, and a few friends, I have come to realize that I am not alone.

I also started thinking about others who may also be struggling with similar emotions. I now recognize that my past experiences and my journey walking through this with Christ's help could help others. The more I have shared my desire to write this book, the more I have been able to see that this is a purpose to which God has called me.

Was it easy to write these chapters? Of course not. After all, I am a history teacher, not an English major. As much as I felt God leading me to share this story, I have often felt fear that I wasn't prepared to do it in a way that would honor my heavenly

Father. My desire to help others by sharing my story is scary. John Eldridge writes about this in his book *Desire*: "To live with desire is to choose vulnerability over self-protection." (p.59) In other words, it is an act of trust and an act of faith. As I began fulfilling my calling, I felt myself doubting my abilities and wondered if I had misunderstood what I thought God was telling me to do. I began praying for guidance and clear signs that I was on the right path and felt justified to continue writing when I received several such indicators.

Mostly, I was worried that my story wouldn't make a difference. As I began putting my story on paper, I looked for confirmation that I could help others. I didn't have to look far to see that many people could benefit from hearing my story. As a high school teacher, I work closely with counselors and hear stories from them and from my students themselves that break my heart. Listening to some of these stories from young girls makes me feel helpless. Some have been homeless, in a broken home, or live with people who don't care about them. I know girls who cut themselves, have attempted suicide, and are very depressed. I wish I could tell every one of them that there is always another option and always someone who can help.

As I thought more about this issue, I realized that in the news across the United States, stories emerge daily about sexual assault in a college setting. In fact, a recent poll of college students nationwide, published in *The Washington Post* (June 12, 2015), found that twenty-five percent of female students reported being sexually assaulted either through physical force or while incapacitated by drugs/alcohol. And that was just those who reported an assault. How many others never told anyone about the pain they suffered? How many still hear their assailant's voice insisting, "It won't hurt. You'll like it!", as I still do so many years later? I want to reach out to these girls and women. I want to let them know they have a God who loves them and that with His love, they too can find healing and grace.

At New Hope Church, we have a group of people who meet every Friday for a service called Celebrate Recovery. It is designed to help those like me who are healing from hurts, hang-ups and habits. People share stories as part of their own healing, but also to allow others the benefit of knowing they are not alone in their struggles. While my story might be slightly different from that of some other victim, I hope that my story will allow others to lean on God to find hope in the future. It is important to remember we can overcome problems. God will give us grace, and He can transform anything, even a broken life. We just have to have confidence in Him and let Him in.

For myself, I am finding that the more I depend on my faith to get me through the tough times, the easier everything becomes. The Bible says that we don't have to live with our insecurities. Instead we can grow past them. We can be secure in knowing that God is working in us through His divine power, just as He showed His divine power when He raised Jesus from the dead. God calls us from our insecurities to be closer to Him. He gives us the opportunity to walk away from our past. As Romans 8: 9-11 tells us:

"But if God has taken up residence in your life, you can hardly be thinking more of yourself than of Him. Anyone, of course, who has not welcomed this invisible but clearly present God, the Spirit of Christ, won't know what we're talking about. But for you who welcome Him, in whom He dwells (even though you still experience all the limitations of sin), you yourself experience life on God's terms. ***It stands to reason, doesn't it, that if the alive and present God who raised Jesus from the dead moves into your life, He'll do the same thing in you that He did in Jesus, bringing you alive in himself?*** When God lives and breathes in you, you are delivered from that dead life. With the spirit living in you, your body will be as alive as Christ's!" (MSG)

I like to refer to that scripture when someone shares a personal problem or hardship that has left them feeling lost and asks me,

"Now what?" The truth is that when we live with God in us, He helps us put our problems to rest, and when we listen to God, we are able to move on. I believe that God doesn't use us in spite of our weaknesses. Rather He uses us because of those weaknesses. Accepting this gives us courage and strength to get past whatever we are going through.

So hold on to hope. Hold on to your faith. Sometimes on your worse day, your only strength may come from knowing that God loves us despite our unworthiness and brokenness. As Scripture tells us in Romans 5:6-8: "You see, at just the right time, when we were still powerless, Christ died for the ungodly. Very rarely will anyone die for a righteous person, though for a good person someone might possibly dare to die. But God demonstrates his own love for us in this: While we were still sinners, Christ died for us."

EPILOGUE

As for my own story, I hope that my growth in faith can be an example to others. I went from being an unchurched, scared, confused girl to a confident follower of Jesus. This did not happen all at once but over many years of my life, requiring a lot of time and maturity as I tried to heal from the wounds of my past.

As a newly baptized young adult, I searched for answers and understanding of my life. I had many questions, and at times I found myself angry at God for letting me suffer as a child. I now understand that God doesn't cause bad things to happen to people. The Bible explains that the world God created was perfect, free of pain and suffering. Things would have stayed that way if humans had respected and obeyed God.

But God permitted human beings to have free will in deciding how we live. This free will has generated many problems in the world, including poverty, hunger, and war. The Bible presents a future when God will reverse this downward trend. How do we know it will happen? We can look at Jesus' death and resurrection as an example of God's amazing work. When we believe in Jesus, we become a part of the renewal of this world.

I also believe that God will not let bad things happen to good people forever and that He will bring justice to victims and restoration for those who trust in Jesus. God promises us just that in the last book of Revelation:

"Then I saw a new heaven and a new earth, for the old heaven and the old earth had disappeared... I heard a loud shout from the throne, saying, 'Look, God's home is now among His people! He will live with them, and they will be His people. God Himself will be with them. He will wipe every tear from their eyes, and there will be no more death or sorrow or crying or pain. All these things are gone forever." (Revelations 21:1-4, NLT)

I hope that my own story provides hope for the hopeless. Hope is believing that the best is still to come. Hope is knowing that God is in control and that life is full of meaning. The purpose of our lives is found in the redemption story that He has provided to us in Scripture. The apostle Paul speaks of this to the people of Colossae:

"We can't quit thanking God our Father and Jesus our Messiah for you! We keep getting reports on your steady faith in Christ, our Jesus, and the love you continuously extend to all Christians. The lines of purpose in your lives never grow slack, tightly tied as they are to your future in heaven, kept taut by hope." (Colossians 1:3-5, MSG)

So I want others to hear my story, my journey of faith, and understand that it's okay to feel like you don't know what God is doing in your life at a given point. You are not alone. When you lean on others and trust in God, He will see you through your struggles. Each time you do this, you will grow closer to Him.

Perhaps you are like I was and feel like a caterpillar inching along, desperate to learn more about God and understand what it means to have faith. Or maybe you are stuck in your cocoon, yearning for a personal relationship with Jesus. Wherever you are in your journey, please remember my story and trust God. His goodness will triumph in the end.

Like me, you will burst forth from that dark, enclosed chrysalis, transformed into a beautiful new creation.

And you too will fly!

Printed in the United States
By Bookmasters